A HANDBOOK OF HOLISTIC HEALING

LUIS S.R. VAS

A Handbook of Holistic Healing

ST PAULS

Copyright © 2002 The Bombay Saint Paul Society

ST PAULS Publishing
187 Battersea Bridge Road, London SW11 3AS, UK
www.stpauls.ie

First published in UK 2003

ISBN 085439 676 4

Set by TuKan DTP, Fareham, Hampshire, UK
Printed by Interprint Ltd, Marsa, Malta

ST PAULS is an activity of the priests and brothers
of the Society of St Paul who proclaim the Gospel
through the media of social communication

Contents

Introduction	7
The Holistic Healing Approach	9
The Healing Process	13
The Healing Power of Prayer	22
Inner Healing	33
Healing through Visualisation	37
Healing through an Inner Adviser	43
Fast Action Stress Relief	52
Bringing More Health into Everyday Life	59
A Journey to Total Health	64
What Causes Disease?	67
Importance of Good Nutrition	71
Nutritional Therapy	74
Eat According to Your Blood Group	81
How to Calm the Mind with Touch	86
Therapeutic Touch	90
Relaxation through Expanded Awareness	99
The Healing Power of Faith	108
Increase Your Healing Ability	110
Healing Intuition	113

Intuitive Diagnosis	129
How to Befriend Your Pain	134
Are You Continually Fatigued?	137
The Issue of Obesity	140
High Blood Pressure Disorder	144
Ayurvedic Principles and Guidelines	152
The Sleep–Health Link in Ayurveda	159
Uses of Reflexology	166
Handling Asthma	171
Dealing with Acne Holistically	179
Healing through Aura	184
Eye–Body Connection	194
Tension Headaches	199
Ageing Gracefully	203
10 Ways to Better Health Now!	207

Introduction

◆

Modern medicine has been extremely successful in tackling major illnesses like bacterial and viral infections as well as in providing immediate relief to fevers and painful conditions. But its very success has proved its undoing. Antibiotics have killed the weaker strains of germs and stronger ones have come back with a vengeance with which antibiotics are less successful in coping. The AIDS epidemic has yet to find a widely applicable solution. Bypass surgery has proved only a temporary solution for heart blockages, until the next artery gets blocked. In addition to all this, in some parts of the world medical care is becoming expensive to the point of being unaffordable to most patients.

It is not surprising therefore that patients should be on the lookout for alternative cure to their ailments. What is surprising is that allopathic doctors of great repute have pioneered in the search for non-allopathic cures for their patients. Among the most notable are Dr Dean Ornish, who has demonstrated that a change in lifestyle is much more effective than bypass surgery in treating and reversing heart blockages; Dr Larry Dossey, who has shown massive evidence that prayer is a powerful form of treatment for any ailment. Dr Hong Liu, a Chinese allopath, has demonstrated that Qi Gong, a Chinese traditional treatment, is as successful if not more than Western medicine, and can be powerfully combined with allopathic treatments to speed them up; Dr Gerald Epstein incorporated visualisation techniques to speed up his patients' cures in a wide variety of ailments; so did oncologist Dr Carl Simonton who used visualisation in speeding up remission in cancer patients; Dr Herbert Benson of Harvard Medical School demonstrated that certain meditation techniques reduced blood pressure; Dr Juliet Orloff introduced intuition into Western medical treatment... The list is endless.

In this book I have tried to bring together the principles and recommendations of these and other medical practitioners so that readers can benefit from them without extensive reading. I use the term holistic medicine to mean drugless therapy which includes nutritional advice. Although homeopathy can be legitimately considered part of holistic medicine, it is not included here because it involves the taking of prescribed drugs even if in microscopic amounts which patients cannot prescribe for themselves. On the other hand, other than consulting their family physician or a specialist on whether their condition can cope with the exercises, visualisations or meditation techniques prescribed here, patients can then act on their own in following the recommended treatment to speed up the cure, or take it up as a preventive measure.

The techniques prescribed are by no means exhaustive and I would be grateful for advice based on personal or clinical experience of medical practitioners for inclusion in future editions.

I dedicate this book to the Medical Mission Sisters who have been rendering extraordinary service to humanity by bringing holistic healing to those least able to afford any kind of medical treatment.

Luis S. R. Vas

1
The Holistic Healing Approach

There are three basic aspects of the holistic approach to medicine, according to researcher Bobby Jennings. First, disease prevention is emphasised by placing responsibility with the individual as self-healer to use his own resources to promote health, prevent illness and encourage healing. Second, holistic medicine considers the patient as an individual and a unique person, not only as a symptom-bearing organism. Finally, holistic practitioners choose from the many available diagnoses, treatment and health methods, including both alternative and standard medical methods. Contrary to common belief, holistic medicine does not disregard conventional medical practices. In fact, most holistic practitioners view the use of standard medical practices as only one of many ways in which to achieve wellbeing.

Holistic diagnosis can include standard laboratory tests as well as other diagnostic methods, since the interrelated physical, mental and spiritual capabilities in the whole person are major health determinants. A practitioner may, for example, watch the way patients stand, sit and walk, as well as look for the physical expression of an emotional state.

Health-care treatments are usually provided in the context of the patient's culture, family and community. Holistic medicine addresses not only the whole person, but also the person's environment and involves various healing and health-promoting practices. Holistic medicine does not have any single widely used diagnostic procedure or treatment because it is primarily an attitude about health and healing. Thus, traditional physicians, nurses, specialists and other health-care professionals may be holistic practitioners depending on their practices but may often be hard to find by patients seeking a holistic approach. Many times these practitioners embrace the approach but not the label for fear of criticism from their peers. This will change more and more as the public demands to be treated holistically, rather than partially or symptom by symptom.

In recent years a variety of traditionally trained medical professionals have examined the ideals and documented benefits of holistic medicine. Some still criticise the fragmentation of the holistic medical movement and blame it for promoting medical quackery and in some cases this may be true. However, one cannot disregard the existence of "quackery" in the conventional medical establishment as well. Unfortunately there are some persons willing to prey upon the lack of knowledge of others or simply misdiagnose due to tradition. Others, calling for physicians as consolers and healers, as well as technologically trained practitioners, embrace the humanistic approach offered by holistic medicine.

Although many holistic practitioners make use of available technical equipment and statistical analysis, the emphasis is on each patient's genetic, biological and psychosocial strength and uniqueness. Holistic practice is designed to use all known health-related knowledge to mobilise the individual's self-healing capacity. Surgical or medical intervention is not disputed in holistic medical practice, but is de-emphasised as the cure all and end all. Rather, the emphasis is on preventive self-care and self-education.

Holistic medicine's common principle is that patients should be active participants in their own health-care since all individuals are believed to have the mental, emotional, social, spiritual and physical capacity to heal themselves. After years of over-specialisation and use of dehumanising pure scientific practices by the conventional medical establishment, a more common sense approach was of course necessary and inevitable.

In recent times, the family practitioner or general physician has almost disappeared from many medical establishments. Patients were rushed off to specialist after specialist with no one really supervising the overall health of the patient. In recent years, concern has risen over the settings in which health-care takes place. In holistic care, emphasis is placed on out-patient care as opposed to hospital stay except in most warranted cases. Since hospital settings often overwhelm and intimidate, many holistic health-care facilities have been located outside but near conventional hospitals. With this arrangement, specialised hospital personnel and technology are readily available when necessary and the patient can avoid stressful hospital stays.

The use of touch is another major element of holistic medicine. Many body therapies, including massage, chiropractic manipulation and rolfing, or systematic massage, use physical contact. These touch-oriented therapies are based on a holistic approach to human functioning. Touch is used to promote greater relaxation, to improve body alignment and functioning, or to enhance sensory awareness.

Other methods used in holistic medicine may include acupuncture, biofeedback, meditation, modern fluid replacement, ancient energy balance, psychic healing, hypnosis and spiritual and physical disciplines and surgery. But again emphasis must be laid on the whole rather than on just one aspect.

Holistic medicine views health as a positive state, rather than as the absence of disease. Such a positive approach to treating existing diseases is currently being used by many researchers and physicians. This positive-attitude approach to medical care has been used in cancer therapy by having patients think differently and positively about chemotherapy and radiation therapy.

Another holistic health therapy called psychotherapeutic bodywork was first developed by Wilhelm Reich. It has greatly influenced the field of bioenergetics. Once an illness has been identified, it is viewed both as a misfortune and as an opportunity for discovery. Holistic medicine emphasises the idea that psychosocial stresses, such as unemployment, divorce or death of a close relative or friend, may contribute to ill health.

Using a common sense approach, one sees that a patient should be treated using whatever method achieves good results. The conventional medical establishment argues that the existence of "alternative methods" often prevents the patient from seeking standard treatments, and in some cases this may be true. However, medical history has firmly documented many cases of misdiagnosis and mistreatment even by conventional methods.

This is not to say that perfect health is achievable, only that the goal of modern medicine should use the methods that treat the person rather than the disease.

2
The Healing Process

♦

It is important to realise that all healing techniques whether they be physical, energetic, mental or emotional are an attempt to re-establish proper flow, according to Dr José Stevens, Ph.D. Blockage or stoppage has occurred because somewhere, somehow, there has been limited perception. The direction of healing then always moves from the more limited picture to the big picture, from the personality to the essence. The key behind all healing techniques, he says, is intention and focus of attention. Since energy follows thought, all disease is a product of certain thought processes and healing is the result of certain balancing thoughts. Thoughts without the energy of emotion, however, are not result producing. In his book, *Earth to Tao*, he prescribes following the steps to self-healing recommended below:

1. Being present

The most important element of self-healing is the ability to be present with yourself. You cannot begin the process of self-healing while you are preoccupied with mulling over baggage from the past or actively scripting the future. These activities scatter your focus and energy to the extent of rendering you powerless to alter your state. When your focus is blunted and your energy is dissipated by mulling and scripting, you lower your natural frequency in a way that makes you slow to respond. This often shows up as the pseudo-emotion of depression or the non-emotion of apathy. The path of healing requires your reorientation and focus on the present moment of aliveness. However, focusing on the present brings up the true emotion that was being masked or blocked. This usually represents experiencing painful feelings before the release to joy. Therefore it is usually avoided.

Being in the present moment means facing the pain that is based on fear. However, being in the present allows you access to the higher centres for energy and support that were formerly blocked. So, as you face the fear, you become privy to a most powerful set of supports that exists within you at all times.

To become present, pay attention to the sensations in your own body. Since your body is always present, you will be guided by it to be present also. You may not, however, like how it feels. It may be angry with you for abandoning it, or it may be petrified with fear. This you must face if you desire healing. In the event you are in so much emotional or physical pain that you find it impossible to be present, then you need the support of another who can help you to become present more gradually. After all, after a long absence, becoming present can be a shocking experience.

2. Grounding

One excellent method of becoming more present is the process of grounding your energetic system to your immediate locale. Since your body is presently residing on the planet Earth, the earth is the most expedient place to ground to. Here is how it is done:

a. Relax by sitting and sighing deeply several times.
b. Imagine a connection between the base of your spine, the general area of your instinctive centre, and the core of the earth.

c. Strengthen and clear this channel by following it slowly down and then up, once again using the power of your imagination.

d. Use this channel to drain away excess energy and any unwanted condition. Send it downward for recycling.

e. Next, concentrate on energy from the earth rising through openings in the soles of your feet, up your legs, into the base of your spine, and distributing gradually throughout your body. Since the earth is always present beneath your feet, it will have the effect of immediately bringing you into greater focus through your body.

3. Establishing an essence connection

After you have established a sense of grounding to locate and stabilise your body, you are in a position to bring into it a higher degree of essence. Bringing in greater degrees of essence accelerates spiritual growth and awareness, and promotes healing on every level.

Since it is not possible to squeeze the totality of your essence into your physical body, most people bring into their bodies only a fraction of the essence potential available to them. You can raise this amount with an act of will and concentration. However, it is important that you do this incrementally to avoid being overwhelmed. Your body, if habitually subjected to low levels of essence and energy, may regard increase of essence within it as an intrusion and a threat. It must get used to the increases gradually just as you must introduce food slowly after a fast to avoid nausea, or else the body will react in fear and resist essence expression.

Here is a method to raise the level of essence within your body:

a. Imagine a ball of brilliant energy over your head.

Postulate that this represents the totality of your essence, pure potential and infinite energy.

b. Imagine you can draw a brilliant beam or channel of this energy down through a hole in the crown of your head, gradually streaming through your head and face; down your spinal column, branching through your arms and out of your hands; cascading down to the base of your spine meeting the upwelling earth energy there. Create a mix and distribute this mixture gradually throughout your body.

c. Expel the excess energy and unwanted conditions through the base of your spine down into the earth.

d. You have mingled essence here with the physical material that forms your body and comprises your personality. This is the marriage of the sun and the earth. The child is you.

e. As you reach greater levels of comfort with practice, bring in more and more of each stream until you are working with large amounts. Expect an emotional, physical or psychological reaction, so do this slowly over a period of days and weeks or even months, several times a day for five minutes, or a longer sitting of twenty minutes would be sufficient.

f. The increased streams of energy tend to dislodge blocks and obstacles within your energetic system, so that they come to the surface, so to speak, for review. You need not become overly identified with them, a simple acknowledgement will do. However, as these come up, there is a tendency for you to feel that all these old problems have come back to plague you. Many people discontinue the exercise at this point because they fear it is making them worse. Understand that this is part of the process. Presently you will feel better than you ever have before.

g. You may experience physical reactions such as trembling and shaking. If these become too uncomfortable, discontinue and breathe deeply a few times. Bending over from the waist and touching your toes, without locking your ankles, can be of some help. This helps to unblock and dissipate the accumulated energy. If you experience intense physical pain during the exercise, you are most likely trying to go too quickly. Discontinue for the time being and slow down.

h. This method was known to Egyptian spiritual practitioners who derived the technique from even earlier forms.

4. Calling for support

Power animals and helpers from the other planes are an important part of any healing process. Although all healing is self-healing, you do not exist in a vacuum. You are intimately related to members of your entity, your essence twin if you have one, and the many teachers, friends and students you have developed over your lifetime. These relationships exist whether they are in physical form or not. When they are not in a physical body, they are in a unique position to help from within, because they are not distracted by the many challenges of the physical plane.

Therefore when you feel overwhelmed, ill or imbalanced in any way, it is appropriate to ask for help and support. You may not, however, have your lesson removed or resolved for you. What you get is perspective and guidance. The work remains yours to carry out.

To enlist the support of a spirit guide, do the following:

a. Ask for a spirit guide whom you know and trust, or one that is an expert in the situation you are trying to heal. Ask and you will receive.

b. Ask them to help you with some of the healing steps we have outlined so far. Ask them to help you with staying present, grounding, pulling in higher degrees of essence, clearing your aura and so on.

c. Ask them to help you with insights or clarity concerning the condition of imbalance.

d. Always remember to thank them for their help. Do not be concerned about directing their activities or taking charge of the healing operations. If you wish them to move out, simply state this.

5. Bringing in the higher planes for healing

When you have learned how to bring higher degrees of essence into your body you have developed the ability to work with the higher planes.

Astral Plane: Provides help in the form of power animals, devas and some guides that can offer support and guidance of a more practical nature. Help with emotions.

Causal Plane: Provides teachings and philosophies of a higher order similar to this teaching. Help with beliefs.

Akashic Plane: Provides information about future probabilities. Instinctive centre healing.

Mental Plane: Higher intellect. Intuitions about the nature of the universe. Understanding connectedness with all things. Perceiving the truth.

Messianic Plane: Higher emotional. Perceiving the nature and feeling of agape or unconditional love.

Buddhaic Plane: Higher moving. Perceiving and experiencing the nature of energy. Understanding beauty.

Tao: Connecting with all that is.

To contact the other planes for healing, all you need to do is to acknowledge them and ask to feel the energy of that plane. It helps to visualise the "chakra" or energy spot that you wish to bring it through. For example, for a condition of severe self-deprecation or depression, you may wish to visualise the heart chakra. Establish a connection from this chakra to a colour or symbol of your own choice for the messianic plane, centre for higher emotional healing. Channel the energy of agape from the messianic plane through the heart chakra, for a period of one minute or less. A little bit of healing from these planes can go a long way. If you are seriously ill or wounded you may wish to hook up your solar plexus chakra with a symbol for the Buddhaic plane, centre for energetic healing. Again, you need not hold the connection for longer than one minute.

You can see, then, how you can use each plane for healing in its own specific area.

Very occasionally you may wish to connect with the Tao through the crown chakra on the top of your head for a few moments. This will give you a spiritual healing of the highest order. This is the healing of choice at the time of death.

In order to accomplish this, follow the same procedure described above.

Visualise a symbol or globe of brilliant white light for the Tao. Draw a channel between that light and the crown of your head. Funnel that light into your crown for a few moments.

6. Healing with your hands

Your hands are magical instruments in that while they are quite physical, they have astral properties as well. This is because of the chakras that exist in the palms and at all the fingertips.

Your hands, then, are able to mould and direct energy just as they are able to mould and direct physical matter. They are most useful tools in the art and practice of healing. Your hands work in harmony with your intent and your will. Therefore whatever you intend through your thoughts and feelings can be channelled through your hands. This is the process behind the ancient art of the laying on of hands.

Do not hesitate, then, to use your hands in self-healing or when you assist another. Use your imagination and concentration to direct light and colour to different parts of the body and through the various chakras. Use your hands to help the flow of energy through the joints or for clearing obstacles from the aura. Use your hands for soothing or for closing down that which is gaping too wide. Use your hands to send away unwanted thoughts or to help bring in desired beliefs or feelings.

Placing your hands over physical wounds has powerful healing properties. Unfortunately because of your culture's fixation on germs you have been instructed to keep your hands away from injured parts. While it is unwise to touch a gaping wound, it is certainly helpful to pass your hands over it. Many a doctor, masseuse, dentist and even palm reader has effected healing through touch without the conscious knowledge of it.

7. Steps to healing others

Remember that all effective healing is an attempt to help people heal themselves.

1. The first step is to establish communication with the person being healed, both mentally and emotionally. Note that they need not be present physically for you to accomplish this. If they are not present physically it helps to know their name, age, sex and their address or location.

2. Establish a communication link with their instinctive centre. Greet them and ask their permission to work with them. Ground them and bring them into the present.

3. Assess the problem by posing questions and viewing the mental image pictures you receive. You may sense these instead of see them.

4. Attempt to see, sense or feel the problem through the eyes of the client. Walk in their shoes for a moment without identifying with them.

5. Focus your attention on the area of difficulty, not with the intention of increasing its strength, but with the intention of understanding it more completely.

6. When you get a sense of the problem and have assessed it to your satisfaction, begin to use practical images to heal the malady. For example, if something is separated, use tape to fasten it together. If something is bloated or too full, open a tap to drain it. If something is leaking, cork it up. Use your hands even if you are alone.

7. Next, channel healing energy from the various planes, not from your own personality. The best way is through inspired feeling and images of brilliant light. You can both visualise this and direct it with your hands if you wish.

Any tools or steps that you used for self-healing can be applied to others. If you wish, with their permission you can channel higher degrees of their own essence into their chakras or into their crown. You may wish to show them how to do this for themselves.

3

The Healing Power of Prayer

---◆---

Dr Larry Dossey, MD, wrote a book, *Healing Words*, which became a best seller, in which he documented massive research that proves the efficacy of prayer as a cure to illnesses.

He wrote the book when it became obvious to him that there was strong data suggesting that consciousness works not only in our own bodies, on our own behalf, but is what he calls non-local in the world. It can manifest outside an individual's body. So when we look at the effects of consciousness we have to go beyond looking at the effects of *our* mind on *our* body. His books, including *Healing Words*, have explored this expression of consciousness through distant or intercessory prayer which involves the ability of your consciousness to make an impact on my body at a distance through prayer when I may not even know that you are doing this.

These ideas seem outrageous in the context of modern science but Dr Dossey thinks that there is significant experimental evidence that these phenomena in fact take place and that they are relevant for health.

When he discovered a study in 1988 showing that if people who were really sick, for instance in the coronary care unit, were prayed for unknown to them, they got better – according to a randomised, controlled, prospective, matched double blind study – he went to the [scientific] literature. "If you do this," he says, "you may be shocked at what you can find. There are as many as

150 studies showing, statistically speaking, that there is an effect of distant intercessory prayer."

Dr Dossey began to ruminate about the implications of this discovery. His conclusion was that the significance of this effect lies far beyond whether, when you pray for someone, the cancer goes away, or heart disease heals – that is terrific; but the implications are shocking compared to *that*. What is involved, that some aspect of the consciousness can reach out beyond the body irrespective of space and make this kind of difference? He thinks that there are simply things that consciousness can mediate or do that the brain or the body is incapable of. This is a way of saying that the mind is *more* than the brain and the body.

There is also evidence, he says, that the mind can violate not just spatial separation but also temporal divisions and barriers. There is evidence, he claims, that the mind can reach back into time and reconfigure events at the quantum level which have not yet been observed even though we presume that they have already happened.

This may sound outrageous to somebody who encounters this statement for the first time. But one can be sobered by looking at the experimental evidence. If you reason all of this through, Dr Dossey says, you can easily come to a place where you say, "There's some quality of our mind and consciousness that's simply outside of space and time." If you go to this line of thinking in conclusion, he says, you have reinvented the idea of the soul. In the West, at least, the soul is some aspect of who we are that doesn't die, it has no beginning and no end. And this is basically the quality that we see flowing out of these kinds of experiments.

Dr Dossey admits we do not have a "soul meter" yet. "We can't plug into somebody and get a direct read-out of whether or not they've got a soul. But if you look at the implications of these experiments, I think they clearly point to a soul-like quality in human beings. It seems to me that the implications are absolutely wonderful and magnificent. Great implications for immortality, for eternity – the idea that it isn't all over with the physical death of the brain and body. These implications, it seems to me, dwarf whatever practical value prayer might have. If we pray and we get better, I think that's terrific – we ought to use prayer in that way. But if you pray and the cancer gets *worse* and you die, you may just have to settle for immortality!"

Dr Dossey points out that there are several kinds of prayer: "The two main divisions that I would want to bring out are petitionary prayer, where you petition for something for yourself. You pray for something for *you*. And then there's this more outrageous kind of prayer, which has been called intercessory prayer or prayer at a distance for someone else."

When you pray for yourself, a lot of things happen. Setting aside for the moment whether or not God or a supreme being might be involved in petitionary prayer when you pray for yourself, we know that certain things happen. You think *positively*. And positive thoughts are not confined to your brain. They set in motion a chain of events that has been defined physiologically. The expectation and suggestion achieve a lot of fabulous changes in the immune system and probably every other organ in the body.

When you get into a meditative, prayer-like, contemplative frame of mind the metabolism slows down, the immune system is refreshed, the blood pressure and heart rates subside, blood lactate level falls, and oxygen consumption and carbon dioxide production are diminished. A lot of changes happen, the result of which is that the body becomes healthier. We are not totally in the dark about some of these physiological effects.

"Most people probably aren't interested in that level," Dr Dossey believes. "They want to know, 'When I pray, does it work or not?' I think that if you look at the evidence, you can resoundingly say, 'Yes! This has a healing effect and here's the laboratory proof for that.'"

The bottom line, he stresses, is that prayer is *good* for people. We have always had problems in science saying this. But there is profound and compelling evidence that this is so. When people pray, good things happen to the body. Does the disease always go away? Of course not. Nothing is 100 per cent. But it can be shown that, statistically speaking, prayer has a powerful, healthful effect on the body.

Dr Dossey points out that prayer takes many forms. "Many people follow the formalities of the great religions and pray explicitly for specific events to occur. Some people pray to a personal God or Goddess the Almighty, or Supreme Being; others to an impersonal universe or the Absolute. Others do not pray in a conventional sense but live with a deeply interiorised sense of the sacred. Theirs could be called a spirit of prayerfulness, a sense of simply being attuned or aligned with 'something higher'."

Dr Dossey mentions the case of Herbert Benson of Harvard University Medical School who was a pioneer medical researcher in the study of health benefits of meditation and prayer. He started by studying meditators of the Transcendental Meditation movement. The study showed that when these meditators used a mantra (an oriental word with no meaning for the meditator) healthy bodily changes occurred in them – lower blood pressure, slower heart rate and lower metabolic rates.

Although Transcendental Meditation prescribed secret mantras to its practitioners, Benson believed that there was nothing magical about it and tested his belief by teaching people to use the word "one" or any other phrase they were comfortable with as their mantra. He asked Catholics to use mantra phrases like: "Hail Mary full of grace" or "Lord Jesus Christ have mercy on me". Jews usually used the peace greeting "Shalom" or "Echad" signifying "one". Protestants tended to select phrases like "Our Father who art in heaven" or "the Lord is my Shepherd". Tests showed that all the mantras worked equally effectively in generating the healthy physiological changes in the body which Benson termed relaxation response. But Benson also discovered that those who used the word "one" or similar neutral phrases did not persist with the programme while others who used prayer phrases did. Benson also found the connection between exercise and prayer. He asked runners to repeat a mantra as they ran and discovered that their bodies became more efficient. Before long groups of runners and walkers were practising "aerobic prayer", short mantras keeping time with their steps.

Benson's research demonstrated not only that prayer is a healthy activity for the body but that people's selection of prayer methods varies greatly. It also revealed that prescribing one right way to pray can be discouraging to people and results in prayer drop outs. Just as there are personality types there are also spiritual types that are comfortable with some types of prayer and not with others.

Dr Dossey even discovered that dream prayer is possible. He quotes from the book *Prayer: Finding the Heart's True Home*, by Richard J. Foster: "When the Spirit has come to reside in someone, that person cannot stop praying; for the Spirit prays without ceasing, in him. No matter if he is asleep or awake, the prayer is going on in his heart all the time. He may be eating or drinking, he may be resting or working – the incense of prayer will ascend spontaneously from his heart. The slightest stirring of his heart is like a voice which sings in silence and in secret to the Invisible."

Dr Dossey writes about the Spindrift Organisation which has conducted studies in the laboratory showing that prayer works. After proving that prayer is effective they proceeded to investigate which type of prayer strategy works best. One of the most important contributions is the distinction they make between directed and non-directed prayer. Practitioners of directed prayer have a specific goal image or outcome in mind. They may be praying for cancer to be cured, the heart attack to resolve itself, or the pain to go away. Non-directed prayer in contrast is an open-ended approach in which no specific outcome is held in mind. It is important always to bear in mind that the most important discovery of the Spindrift tests is that prayer works and that both methods are effective. But in these tests the non-directed technique appeared quantitatively more effective, frequently yielding results that were twice as great or more when compared to the directed approach.

Dr Dossey adds: "An obvious question arises concerning non-directed prayer: if one does not pray for a specific result how can one tell if the prayer is answered? Spindrift believes, on the basis of a large number of tests, that when a non-directed prayer is answered, the outcome is always in the direction of what is best for the organism."

Science, Dr Dossey maintains, is terrific at showing whether or not something happens. For instance, does distant intercessory prayer have an effect? Science is great at answering that. And we are giving a yes answer to that. He is less enthusiastic, however, about whether or not we are ever going to be able to come to a full understanding about how that actually happens. For instance there are phenomena in modern physics at the level of quantum physics – the understanding of the very small, the subatomic domain – where we see things that clearly happen, but we do not have a clue about how they happen. There is an area called Belts' theorem, where you separate two electrons to fantastic distances and you change one and, instantly, the other one changes. There is no time for a signal to pass between them. How does one know when the other is changing? We don't have a clue. But scientists acknowledge that this happens in experiment after experiment.

The same thing happens with distant intercessory prayer, Dr Dossey claims. How on earth does it take place? It is probably inconceivable to most scientists how it happens. We have occasions in science to acknowledge the phenomenon and to honour its existence without even having a theory and an understanding about how it happens. He believes we will acknowledge that many of these so-called miracles occur without a full understanding of why. "I'm sort of a science junkie and I'd love to have the reasoning behind all of this. We may be a long time in getting it, if ever."

In the 1970s you tended to be looked at very peculiarly when you used the words "mind" or "consciousness". But all that has changed. As a single example: biofeedback was thought to be a radical, blasphemous thing to do then. Nobody raises an eyebrow about biofeedback any more. Look at the change that has happened recently in alternative therapies for heart disease. Dean Ornish, MD, has discovered a complementary way to reverse heart disease – which kills more Americans than all other diseases combined – without surgery. When Ornish started doing this work a few years ago, doctors laughed at him. Now, the debate has completely switched. Nobody argues about it any more. They argue about the fine points of the diet that's involved.

Doctors have come around in a major way to saying consciousness not only matters, it matters a lot. We are talking matters of life and death here. Unfortunately, a lot of physicians still have their heels dug in; they are not prepared to look at evidence.

There are two factors involved. One is that we need better and more evidence. That clearly would help, as evidenced by the experience of Dr Ornish, who came up with a bullet-proof scientifically designed study showing that consciousness (meditation), oil-free vegetarian diet and walking exercise can reverse heart disease. So the evidence clearly helps. We need more of it, Dr Dossey says.

When Philippe Semmelweiss proposed, in the 1830s in Vienna, that it would be a good idea if doctors washed their hands before they delivered babies, and he instituted a programme of hand washing, he brought down dramatically the death rate in the maternity ward where people washed their hands. In spite of the evidence, the doctors ridiculed Semmelweiss and they hounded him out of Vienna. He fled to Budapest. Finally, his life was made so miserable because of this apparently blasphemous idea that he committed suicide.

You say, "Well, that was in the 1830s in Vienna. We would never do that here today." It is not true. We do it all the time. Doctors can be looking at the evidence right in front of their faces and claim not to see it. And sometimes when they look at it, they say, "Yes, this is compelling," then they drop back to the old ways and continue to criticise. We need to do better. We need to be more open-minded.

Politicians have noted the interest in alternative medicine and are trying to figure out how they can use it. There are votes there. One third of the total medical schools in the USA now are developing courses in alternative therapies. This is a dramatic turnaround and it is extraordinarily rapid. We are at that place in the curve where it begins to shoot up exponentially as far as change and openness are concerned. "I think the change is occurring so fast that few people can keep up with what is really happening in this field of alternative therapies."

"For a long time," Dr Dossey confesses, "I've been attentive to the impact of consciousness and health and have honoured that in various ways in my own life. For a very long time I've had an active life of contemplation. I prefer to use the word 'contemplation' because when one uses the word 'meditation', it has a foreign ring to it. That is unfortunate because I think that these activities are universal. I regularly make space in my life, in my daily routine, for calming my mind and body and setting time aside and getting quiet. For many years I had a morning prayer ritual in my office where I would ask for the greater good for my patients whom I was about to see that day. I really can't conceive of my life operating very well without these kinds of activities – setting aside time to *listen*, to not do; to just *be*. To be open to whatever messages the universe wants to visit on me. Diet's very important for me. After growing up on a beef diet in central Texas cattle country I think my family there would probably be ashamed to see my diet these days. Exercise is utterly essential to me. I'm a fanatical exerciser and it's really important because of travel schedules and being in hotels and aeroplanes and living on the road. All of these things are really important to me. I almost hate to talk about them, though, because people then wonder what the magic formula is. 'If it works for old Dossey, maybe I'd better be doing that.' That's the risk of people in our position talking about what we do. People tend to think that it is engraved in stone and it is not. I wouldn't offer any of my regimen as a formula for anyone."

Dr Dossey recalls how, after years and years of reading about the tenets of Oriental philosophies including Buddhism, Taoism and Hinduism, he was shocked to discover through the books of Evelyn Underhill, famous English mystic, that there was an equally majestic, mystical tradition within Western Christianity. He thought all of that happened somewhere east of the Suez Canal. The Western mystical tradition was certainly a very refreshing discovery, he comments.

In the *Journal of Scientific Exploration*, Dr Dossey discloses, a biologist from an American university proposed a new aesthetic for science based not on measurement, analysis and objectivity but on – guess what – *love*. He says that unless we have a compassionate interaction with the universe, we cannot see the pattern; we will forever be blind to the way the universe displays itself holistically unless we fall in love with it.

"If we *were* able to bring these kinds of emotions and attitudes to our science, I think the universe would open up to us in wondrous ways that we've been blind to recently. And I'm hopeful that we are moving in that direction and my interaction with scientists here and there tells me that many scientists indeed are. Pierre Teilhard de Chardin, the Jesuit priest and palaeontologist, said once, 'Research is the highest form of adoration.' That says a lot for me. It is possible to do science with a sense of reverence and a sense of sacredness. That's what we need to be doing."

Dr Dossey's book *Prayer is Good Medicine* discusses questions about the nature of prayer. What is prayer? What is it good for? What's the evidence? Should I be doing it? How do you pray? It's a response to questions that are on people's minds. Another book is on what he considers to be the shadow side of prayer, what he calls negative prayer. It looks at the possibility that through our thoughts, emotions and intentions, we can not only help people as through prayer but we can also hurt them. There's substantial evidence in real life and in the laboratory that we can harm other living creatures at a distance when they are unaware of it. "It's a look at a very uncomfortable subject for a lot of people but it's one I think we would be foolish to ignore."

"As I looked in my own life I realised that one of my reasons for exploring these areas is to try to heal a gap, a breach, in my own life which I think a lot of other people experience also: the schizophrenic division between your spiritual side – your intuitive side – and your intellect. We've learned in this culture that you supposedly can't get these things together. But I think we can. And I think we'd better, because if we don't, the outlook for this world is pretty bleak. I'm confident that if we really pay attention to some of these cutting edge areas in science, such as the evidence for prayer and the spiritual implications of these studies and experiments, we will be provided with a way to harmonise the two vectors in our psyche, our mind and our being – the intellect, the rational and the logical with the spiritual and the intuitive. I think this is a healing that we seriously need because that split has caused immense pain for untold numbers of people in our culture. I think we're on the verge of healing that split."

A Prayer for Prayer
by Larry Dossey

May we let prayer be.

May we allow it to follow
the infinite patterns of the human heart.

May we learn to practise the most difficult art,
the art of non-interference.

May we be guided by prayer
instead of attempting to guide prayer.

May we allow prayer to be what it needs to be,
to be what it is.

May we let prayer be.

4
Inner Healing

◆

For more than two decades Sr Mary Usha, SND, author of *Hidden Springs to Healing* and *A Time for Healing*, has been engaged in the practice of inner healing in which she blends elements of psychotherapy, transactional analysis and her own experience as a Catholic nun. In her books she describes some of these techniques. For example she maintains that physical illnesses can have emotional root causes. Some of these are given below with the respective emotional causes in brackets.

Areas of physical pain:

1. Head, eyes, ears, sinuses (resentment, lack of forgiveness, guilt, fear, doubt, anxiety)
2. Nose, mouth, throat, neck, upper back and shoulders (hostility, negativity, holding back feelings of rejection)
3. Heart, lungs, chest. Including palpitation, blood pressure and blood disease (envy, despair, lack of forgiveness, discouragement, sense of inferiority, fear, anger, enmity)
4. Stomach, intestines, lower back (sorrow, suppressed grief, suppressed lack of forgiveness)
5. Reproductive organs (sexual tensions and urges)
6. Legs, knees and feet (feelings of insecurity, anxiety and instability).

Among the exercises she suggests for the inner healing of these ailments is the following: "Quieten yourself and relax enough so that you can go back in memory through your own life history. In the light of your present burdens – negative emotions and feelings, chronic illnesses and painful memories – ask yourself in the presence of God which of these burdens you would now want to get rid of. Recall to mind the people who knowingly or unknowingly were involved in these traumatic events, the memories of which are still painful to you. With the power of God's grace and with firm determination give unconditional forgiveness to any and every person whom you perceive to have hurt you. Then ask forgiveness from them if you have hurt them in any way, or have kept grudges or resentment or anger towards them, consciously or unconsciously. Thank the Lord for freeing you and these people; thank him for giving you and them his peace."

The effect of a life story upon health and interpersonal relations

Sr Mary Usha discovered that using well-known stories from childhood and their characters with which you identify most is helpful in healing painful memories as well as interpersonal problems. She found that stories like Little Red Riding Hood, The Tortoise and the Hare, The Monkey and the Crocodile help people in healing themselves through the following exercise: "Jot down the story from your childhood which made the biggest impression on you. Do not worry whether you have objectively remembered all the details as they are in the book or as someone told you; tell the story as you like it told, as you think it should be told. Next, analyse the character in the story that has struck you most, with whom you identify best, whose role you play effectively.

Finally check out and see the parallel in your own life. Do you in fact, whether consciously or unconsciously, live out a given role from the childhood story? Do you do this freely or compulsively? Are you happy with the results or unhappy? If you can now change the story you can rewrite the script giving it a different ending altogether. You can do this with the freedom of a loved child of God. You are not condemned to be a carbon copy of a story character; be yourself and relate to others as you want to, not as the story would make you. Reconciliation in the power of God gives you the freedom to do this."

Dreams as gifts from God

Sr Mary Usha believes that dreams are the real thermometer of our spiritual life and that they come at critical moments. They are God's gifts, she writes, but they need "reading", interpreting. She gives some of the interpretations of dream symbols that she came to recognise early. We give them below with their interpretation in brackets:

- Climbing a mountain (an inner struggle to conquer my "mountain" of anger or other obstacles within me)
- Jumping down or flying away (I want to get away from a painful situation)
- Swimming peacefully, boating calmly (I am happy, secure in my environment)
- Flying a plane (I am out of touch with reality or else not on good terms with those on the "ground")
- Making a mess in public (I am making a mistake in front of others and I want to hide it, cover it up, blame others)

- Sleeping with the other sex (I want to share myself, my views; I want support and closeness from others)
- Searching frantically (I am in a desperate situation and I need help)
- Travelling by public transport (at my subconscious level I am trying to hear what others are saying about me)
- Travelling on a bicycle (I am in touch with my environment and in control. I can stop at any time; I can go at my own pace)
- Moving in a forest or jungle (I am feeling unsafe, lost)
- Travelling by train (I am anxious about many things)
- Giving birth (I am a child again)
- Deaths and funerals (someone in my life is gone and I am a new creation, at a new beginning)
- Known/unknown persons and places (these represent the known and unknown character traits of my own personality).

Sr Mary Usha suggests the following exercise to help you unravel the meaning of your dreams: "Write down one of your recent dreams. Then take each element of it. Let it, like a person, speak to you, telling you about yourself. Each element is a part of you and your personality. See what new dimensions of yourself you discover by such interpretation. Let this be a prayerful exercise in the power of God."

5
Healing through Visualisation

---◆---

Gerald Epstein was a traditional psychiatrist until 1974 when he spent six weeks in Israel as a visiting professor in law and psychiatry at Hadassah Medical School. Here this practising Freudian psychoanalyst met a young man who had undergone three years of psychoanalysis, five times a week, to cure himself of chronic depression – to no effect. After all these years he went to a woman who practised waking dream therapy, another term for visual imagery. After four sessions with her once a week, he considered himself cured within a month. His curiosity aroused, Epstein met the young man's therapist, Madame Colette Aboulker-Muscat. Dr Epstein later claimed that this meeting changed his life after learning what waking dream therapy was. It is a "deep experiential journey of inner life, using a person's night dreams or daily conversation as the starting point for waking exploration". Dr Epstein developed his own imagery exercises which became a form of waking dreams – "dreams that can make reality". Dr Epstein incorporated them in his book, *Healing Visualisations: Creating Health through Imagery.*

Dr Epstein later recalled: "My clinical experience of the past fifteen years has borne witness not only to the effect of mind on body but to the power of mental imagery to help heal the body... the conditions that I have successfully helped patients treat using mental imagery include rheumatoid arthritis, enlarged prostate, ovarian cyst, inflammatory breast carcinoma, skin rash, haemorrhoids and conjunctivitis."

In his book Epstein mentions that Sigmund Freud successfully used imagery to treat a fourteen-year-old boy suffering from a physical tic, after treating him in only one session. He stresses that it is ironic that "there is not one successfully completed case of psychoanalytic treatment reported by Freud in the twenty-five volumes of his published writings; it was the *only* successful completed treatment mentioned in the twenty-five volumes of Freud's published writings and the only time Freud used imagery as a therapeutic technique." The irony is that thereafter Freud ceased to use imagery in his therapy.

Dr Epstein considers us all gardeners engaged in developing our reality gardens: "As gardeners we have special functions, primarily weeding, seeding and of course harvesting... Mental imagery is a technique for clearing out the old negative weed beliefs and replacing them with new positive beliefs. By becoming a gardener of your own reality self-healing becomes possible."

To demonstrate the impact of imagery work Epstein describes the case of a friend suffering from a bad cold who asked for help with an imagery exercise. This is the exercise he prescribed, called the river of life: "Close your eyes. Breathe out three times to relax yourself. See your eyes becoming clear and very bright. Then see them turning around and looking inwards, becoming two rivers flowing down into the nasal cavity and throat, their flow removing all the waste products, soreness and stuffiness. The rivers flow through your chest and abdomen into your legs, and come out as black or grey strands that you see getting buried deep into the earth. See your breath coming out as black air and see your waste products emerging from below. Sense the rivers pulsating rhythmically through your body and see light coming from above filling up all the cavities in the nose and throat, leaving all the tissues pink and healthy. When you sense both the rhythmic flow and the light filling these cavities breathe out and open your eyes."

Dr Epstein asked his patient to do this exercise every three hours for no more than three to five minutes until his cold cleared up. The patient reported back that he had done the exercise for only one day and promptly recovered.

In another case which Dr Epstein reports a friend had broken her wrist. It had been set by an orthopaedist who had told her that it would require three months to heal. Dr Epstein suggested that she do the following exercise termed "weaving the marrow": "Close your eyes, breathe out three times and see the ends of the bones as they look now. See the two ends touching each other. See and sense the marrow flowing from one end into the other. See this white marrow carried in blue channels of light flowing through the red bloodstream, seeing the arterioles flowing back and forth between the two ends forming a woven net that brings the two ends closer. See the two ends knitting together perfectly until you can no longer see any sign of a break. Know that the bone is now one and open your eyes."

Dr Epstein instructed his friend to do the exercise every three to four hours for up to three minutes each time. After three weeks the friend went to see the orthopaedist who found that the bone had healed completely. He was extremely surprised but could not explain such rapid results.

In his book Dr Epstein notes four aspects which he considers essential for preparing the mind for healing through imagery: intention, quieting, cleansing and changing.

1. **Intention** is what we wish to achieve, for example

healing the cold, setting the bone, getting rid of a tumour.

2. **Quieting** is of two types: (a) external quiet which helps us to concentrate on the task of moving inward. This means avoiding unsettling noises, but certain other sounds like birds, sounds of weather or even a distant hum of traffic could help the process; (b) internal quiet is attained through relaxation brought about through conscious breathing out.

3. **Cleansing**. Every imagery exercise need not involve cleansing but Dr Epstein considers cleansing to be "one of the most important first steps in opening yourself to becoming whole..." To heal ourselves we must begin by "cleaning up our act... by using images we can clear away our denials that something is wrong, clean up our delusions and shine a light on our habitual destructive patterns. Then we can meet our ailments in person and heal ourselves... An imaginary cleansing exercise is also a wonderful way to prepare yourself for the day."

4. **Changing** involves "letting go" of things, ideas, preconceptions about ourselves or others. To feel better involves actively letting go of the desperation involved in identifying ourselves with fixed limited experiences, things and situations dictated by the past.

The procedure for visualising is as follows:

   i. Sit in what Dr Epstein calls the Pharaoh posture. That is, sit in a straight-backed chair that has arm rests with your back straight, arms resting comfortably on the arm rest, hands open, palms either up or down as convenient, and feet flat on the floor. Neither your hands nor your feet should be crossed during this period nor in contact with any other part of the body.

   ii. State your intention for doing the exercise, for

example curing a cold, getting rid of a headache, speeding up the healing of a fracture.

iii. Close your eyes.

iv. Breathe out and let the breathing in happen naturally. Breathing out should be long and slow and the breathing in whatever way it happens.

v. Begin your specific breathing exercise. Although Dr Epstein prescribes specific exercises for specific ailments, there is one called Egyptian healing which is a powerful general aid in self-healing. It is as follows: Close your eyes and breathe out three times. Then imagine yourself standing in a large open field of green grass. See yourself stretching up towards the bright golden sun in a cloudless blue sky. See your arms becoming very long, stretching, palms up towards the sun. The sun's rays come into your palms and circulate through your palms and fingers and beyond the fingertips so that there is a ray beyond each fingertip. If you are right-handed, at the end of each ray of the fingers of your right hand see a complete small hand. At the end of each ray of the fingers of your left hand, see an eye. There are five hands and five eyes. If you are left-handed, see the fingers on your left, the eyes on your right.

Now turn these hands and eyes towards your body and use the eyes to see your way through your body emitting light into or on the area you are investigating so that you can see what you are doing. In the small hands you can use a golden bristled brush for cleaning, laser light tubes for healing, golden scalpels for surgery, cans of golden or blue golden ointment for healing, as well as gold thread for sewing. After finishing your work, come out of your body by the same route as you went in. Any waste materials you took away with the small hands should be thrown away behind you. Hold your hands up towards the sun and let the small hands and eyes retract into your palms to be stored there for future use. Then open your eyes. Remember that this exercise is purely imaginary and should take place only in your mind but working with your inner subjective reality will change your physical reality.

Here are two more suggestions from Dr Epstein for relieving anger and emotional distress:

- Anger directed at oneself or others, if persistent, can have considerable impact on one's health and wellbeing. Epstein suggests the exercise which he terms the noose of anger with the intention of relieving anger. It should be done every time you experience anger, for a duration of three minutes. The procedure is as follows: "Close your eyes; breathe out three times. Remove the noose that is constricting you. At each knot – a noose has up to thirteen knots – see what is causing your anger and correct it (by changing the situation in your mind). Don't allow yourself to mix in other emotions in this exercise; concentrate on anger alone. After finishing all the knots open your eyes, knowing that the anger is gone."

- Emotional distress by Epstein's definition includes confusion, disorganisation, lack of focus and terror. Do the following exercise with the intention of having the particular emotion disappear. It should be done for one to three minutes, every fifteen or thirty minutes when you are experiencing it, until the emotion is cleared. The procedure is as follows: "Close your eyes and breathe out once. In whatever way is appropriate go to your emotion and see the image associated with it. The first step is not to give in to the emotion. Don't be intimidated or scared by it but confront it as if it was a naughty child. Know that what happens in this confrontation will relieve you. Open your eyes when finished."

6
Healing through an Inner Adviser

◆

Dr Martin L. Rossman MD has written a book titled *Healing Yourself*, in which he has presented a step by step programme for better health through imagery. He claims it can be helpful in solving 90 per cent of the problems that people bring to a primary care doctor. He cautions, however, that the self-healing techniques he teaches may enable you to be more independent of medical care but are not a substitute for it. He adds that using self-healing techniques without making a careful assessment of your condition can be dangerous and even life-threatening. Dr Rossman learnt some of these techniques from a physician named Irving Oyle who, instead of routinely prescribing medicines, would have his patients relax and visualise themselves healing, or have them imagine having a conversation with a wise figure who would tell them why they were sick and what they could do to get better.

Dr Rossman comments that healing may not be just a matter of imagining that a problem has disappeared and having it disappear. Imagery may assist a patient in becoming aware of how symptoms have a reason, and lead to changes in attitude or behaviour that finally lead to recovery.

Dr Rossman asserts that through imagery you can stimulate changes in many body functions usually considered inaccessible to conscious influence. "A simple example: touch a finger to your nose. How did you do that? You may be surprised to learn that nobody knows."

That is, no one knows how you go from thinking about touching your nose to triggering the neurological chain effect that will lead your hand to touch the nose.

Likewise you can make yourself salivate but you will probably not find it as easy and some may not be able to do it at all. That is because the autonomic nervous system does not respond easily to abstract thoughts like "salivate" but it does respond to imagery. If you imagine licking a lemon you would have no problem in salivating. Dr Rossman points out that "imagery of various types has been shown to affect heart rate, blood pressure, respiratory patterns, oxygen consumption, carbon dioxide elimination, brainwave rhythms and patterns, electrical characteristics of the skin, local blood flow and temperature, gastrointestinal motility and secretions, sexual arousal, levels of various hormones and neurotransmitters in the blood and immune system function. But the healing potential of imagery goes far beyond simple effects in physiology. Imagery is a natural language of a major part of the nervous system. The right part of our brain has a special relationship not only to imagery, but to emotions." So, Dr Rossman says, if you are ill, you have undoubtedly thought long and hard about why you fell ill and what you need to get better. But this is logical thinking handled by the left brain. And if it has not given you satisfactory answers, good enough to cure your illness, why not get a second opinion from your right brain which is likely to know more about your body, your feelings, your life?

Dr Rossman stresses that when you use imagery, the purpose is not to generate pretty pictures in your mind. It is to pay attention to what your body/mind is trying to tell you. "Imagery is a vehicle to this understanding, which may come through inner pictures, words, thoughts, sensations, or feelings." Dr Rossman asserts that body relaxation is an antidote to the taxing effects of unrelieved stress which is a significant factor in most modern-day illnesses. Dr Rossman cites the following reasons for building a healing foundation on body relaxation:

1. Learning to relax helps develop your confidence in your ability to control your body feelings and thoughts. You realise you have more choices in how to react and how to feel.

2. Body relaxation helps you realise what things, people and thoughts generate tension in you. This is the first step in being able to deal with them effectively.

3. Relaxation disrupts the negative thought patterns you may be habitually producing. It clears your mind and opens it to new ideas, new opportunities and new approaches to solving old problems. You learn how to use your intuition and creativity to move in the direction of your choice.

4. When you are deeply relaxed you get into a state of mind in which more advanced and specific techniques become most effective.

Meeting with an imaginary inner adviser, according to Dr Rossman, is a way of making your own intuitive and creative guidance available to you. He defines intuition as the "power of knowing" without recourse to reason and believes it can be perceived as inner seeing, inner listening and inner feeling.

How can an inner adviser help you? First, according to Dr Rossman, by enabling you to understand more about the nature of your illness, your part in causing it as well as your part in your eventual recovery. Second, an inner adviser becomes a source of support and comfort, bringing a sense of peace, inner calm and compassion in your meetings with your inner adviser. Third, working with an adviser can result in the direct relief of symptoms and recovery from illness. "You may find it reassuring to know that while you do want to know what your adviser has to say, you don't have to do whatever it recommends. Whatever comes from your talk with your adviser you will consider it carefully in the 'clear light of day' and take a good look at what it might mean to act on that advice." Dr Rossman however cautions that if you make a bargain with your adviser, you should make sure that you keep it. That is because you are dealing with a part of yourself here, which you disregard only at a price. Dr Rossman also discloses that there may be times when your inner guide may be either unwilling or unable to give you immediate relief as a sign. In that case he suggests that you ask it what needs to happen prior to receiving some such relief. "This will often start you on the road that eventually leads to the relief you seek." It is advisable not to have expectations of any kind as they are likely to prevent you from benefiting from the experience as much as you would otherwise. "If you are expecting a transcendent experience and a frog jumps into view, you might not recognise it as a potential inner adviser," according to Dr Rossman.

Despite all these preliminary cautions, Dr Rossman maintains that meeting your inner adviser is a simple process. "The first step is to let yourself relax and go to your special inner place. When you are comfortable, quiet and relaxed there, allow an image to appear for your inner adviser. Accept whatever image comes – regardless of whether it is familiar or not. Take some time to observe it carefully and invite it to become comfortable with you, just as if it were real. After all it is a real imaginary figure! Ask your adviser its name, and let it have a voice to answer you. You may hear the name in your mind or you may just understand its name – let yourself 'play along' and accept whatever comes to mind. It is important not to edit or second guess the imagery at this stage. Take some time to become comfortable in the presence of your inner adviser, and as you grow more familiar with it, observe how it seems to be wise and kind. Notice how you feel in its presence. If it feels comfortable to you ask your adviser if it would be willing to help you and let it respond. If it is willing, speak about your problem or illness and ask if it can tell you what you need to know or do to get better. Let it answer you and stay open and receptive to the answers that come."

If you are still unaware of receiving answers to your questions from your adviser, Dr Rossman suggests some other ways to begin the process of dialogue with your inner wisdom:

1. Imagine what your adviser would be like if you did have an adviser.

2. Draw or sculpt the ideal inner adviser with crayons on paper or clay or whatever other material you find suitable.

3. Imagine having a talk with a very good friend in which you tell your friend everything you can possibly tell about your illness, including thoughts and feelings, without holding anything back. Alternatively imagine that your friend has the same problem as you down to the smallest detail and imagine him or her telling you about it and asking for your advice. What advice would you give?

4. Think of an historical or mythological figure that fits your idea of what an inner adviser would be.

5. Write a letter to your wisest self. Ask the questions that are most important to you about your situation, your hopes and fears. Having done that, reverse the roles. Imagine you are your wisest self and write a reply to your letter. You can go on corresponding back and forth till you feel sure you have learnt all you can about your situations and options.

In Dr Rossman's experience it sometimes happens that the adviser who emerges in your mind is not wise and helpful but is hostile and punitive. In such cases, Dr Rossman says, "The simplest way to deal with this inner critic is to assert yourself. Tell it that you are in your quiet place to meet with your inner adviser, a loving, caring figure, and that in this special place you are in control." Dr Rossman maintains that cognitive therapists help people become aware of negative inner messages by having them write them down as they occur. "Then a new thought is chosen to replace each self-suggestion. When you notice yourself thinking or repeating your old thought, stop, mentally 'cancel' the thought, and consciously replace it with the new self-affirming thought. Over time the negative thoughts come less frequently and the positive ones begin to come more easily." He warns, however, that it is not always possible to erase any important figure like an inner critic entirely, and it may not even be in your best interest to do so. But it can be set aside for the time being while you establish what he terms a working relationship with a friendly, supportive inner adviser who can become a strong ally. After you have done this, Dr Rossman thinks you will become more familiar with the process of inner dialogue and your adviser can help you now to handle your inner critic effectively.

It sometimes happens that more than one adviser appears in your imagination. This should not bother you since your whole inner mind is an adviser containing a vast amount of information about you and your wellbeing and may want to express those thoughts, feelings and actions through more than one spokesman.

Other than your adviser you may be able to communicate with your symptoms themselves. A simple direct way of understanding your symptoms according to Dr Rossman is to relax and focus your attention on your symptom, allow an image to come to mind that represents that symptom and then have an imaginary conversation with it. Ask it why it is there, what it wants from you, what it needs from you and *what it is trying to do for you*. Here you are dealing with the personal meaning of your symptoms quite apart from the diagnosis you have been given. "Expressing your feelings in imagery can be the beginning of a dialogue and it is possible to express anger, fear or sadness yet allow communication to continue. Adopt the attitude of a good negotiator or arbitrator to find out what the opposing party wants, what it needs, what it will take and what it has to offer if its needs are met. This is the essence of the inner dialogue process and an attitude free of judgement will facilitate this conversation... Your goal is relief of the symptoms or healing of the illness but your approach will be negotiation rather than warfare."

Dr Rossman discloses that while in some situations the imagery itself will have the effects you desire, in many others it will only point you in the direction you need to go. "The process of grounding your insight of using it to make tangible change in your life is the key to converting the imaginary to the real." Without this step your imagery work may remain mere fantasy. Grounding your imagery, that is, making it real, is accomplished through an act of will with the mental faculty by which a person decides upon and controls her own actions and those of others. Skilful will has been defined by Roberto Assagioli, the Italian psychiatrist who founded Psychosynthesis, as the ability to obtain desired results with the least possible expenditure of energy. Thus grounding is accomplished through a process of will in seven steps:

1. clarifying your aim
2. deliberating on the possibilities
3. choosing the one you will pursue

4. affirming your choice
5. planning your actions
6. mentally rehearsing your plan
7. acting.

The first step in the act of grounding is to make it as clear as possible what you want to accomplish, preferably by writing it down as a statement of your goal and then circling the most important word in the sentence.

The second step is to deliberate or brainstorm so as to generate the maximum number of possibilities of achieving your goal. Brainstorming consists of writing down all the ways you can think of accomplishing your purpose, without stopping to edit or evaluate the feasibility of the idea. Your mind is thus freed to express all its ideas and generate new ones.

The third step is to select the best option for you. Usually the easiest option is the best option provided it leads you in your chosen direction.

The fourth step is affirmation, that is, putting your energy behind your choice. It is helpful if you repeat it to yourself a few times when you are alone.

The fifth step is planning, i.e., making a detailed plan which describes exactly how you will go about accomplishing your goal.

The sixth step is a mental rehearsal, which consists of relaxing and imagining yourself carrying out the plan you have created. Such a mental rehearsal will affirm as well as anticipate and remove any obstacles.

The seventh step is putting your plan into action. While putting it into action you may find some resistance within yourself like laziness, other important work, lack of time. If you do so, take the time to explore it and find out why it is there. How do you find out the purpose of your resistance? As you did while listening to your symptoms, let an image form of it and have a conversation with it. Ask it what it is, what it does for you, how it got there, how it feels about the changes you want to make and whether there is a way to meet its needs and yet allow the change to happen. In this way you may be able to understand your resistance and overcome it, and put your plan into action.

7
Fast Action Stress Relief

◆

NLP or Neurolinguistic Programming is the study of success. It is a new field developed in the 1970s in the United States of America, based on a set of very precise ways to identify how someone who is successful is achieving results. Like the related field of psychology, NLP has applications in so many places that you have almost certainly heard of it under other names already. In education, the application of NLP is known as Accelerated Learning. NLP can also be used to study how excellent sportspeople win competitions, how high-achieving managers create winning teams, how healthy people heal from illnesses quickly, or how people with photographic memory achieve total recall.

NLP practitioner Bobby Bodenhamer here uses Doc Lew Childre's book, *Freeze Frame: Fast Action Stress Relief*, to present NLP's techniques to remove stress. He presents the technique as given in the book in quotes. Then under each of the steps, he reviews the model from the NLP perspective:

Step 1

"Recognise the stressful feeling and *'freeze frame'* it. Take time out." This crucial step in the model obviously has given birth to the name "freeze frame". But how does one freeze frame? In NLP we ask a person a series of "how" questions: How do you stress yourself? How does the process of stressing yourself work? If I wanted to do it, how would I replicate your experience? Do you see a picture or a series of pictures; do you run an internal dialogue inside your head; and/or do you feel the stress by accessing certain kinaesthetic or body sensations? How do you do the process of stressing yourself?

The language of the model assumes that everyone runs a movie to stress themselves for freeze frame. Of course, one can have an internal dialogue going on inside one's head and one can freeze frame or just stop the dialogue.

This first step consists of changing the sub-modality (smaller components of pictures, sounds, feelings, smells and taste) from that of a movie to a still picture or from that of an ongoing dialogue to a frozen dialogue just by stopping it. For those of us who have proficiency at running internal dialogues, sometimes we have difficulty in just stopping it. The best method probably involves placing yourself in peripheral vision.

To stress yourself, you usually focus on that which stresses you. In order to do this you will see through tunnel vision (foveal vision) as you focus on the stressor. Try this out for yourself. Get something that causes you stress.

Notice how you focus on it. As you focus on that which stresses you, pay attention to your internal dialogue about the stressor. Continue seeing the stressor but now allow your eyes to go into peripheral vision as you see the room or whatever lies in the background.

Allow your eyes to go peripheral to where you can see both sides of the room and then even imagine what you can see behind you. Do this so you can still see the stressor, but you now see the entire room and even imagine what you see behind you. In other words, you now see the broader perspective. Notice what happens to your internal dialogue. Did it disappear? For most people it does. This technique provides a way to freeze frame on an internal dialogue.

Step 2

"Make a sincere effort to shift your focus away from the racing mind or disturbed emotions to the area around your heart. Pretend you're breathing through your heart to help focus your energy in this area. Keep your focus there for ten seconds or more."

Step 2 involves a critical component widely taught and utilised in NLP. This component comes from our mind's ability to dissociate from anything including a stressor. How does one "shift focus" from a "racing mind or disturbed emotions to the area around your heart"? By shifting focus from the stressor to the heart, one dissociates consciously from the stressor. The basic definition of association/dissociation involves whether or not one sees oneself in a visual memory. If you recall a memory and you see yourself in the picture, you recall yourself dissociated. If you do not see yourself in the memory, then you recall yourself associated. As for your body's response to the memory, you totally relive the movie as if right there. By shifting one's focus from a stressor to one's heart many, not all, will dissociate from the memory if they had unconsciously recalled the memory associated. In any case, a form of dissociation will take place.

Important also, from the NLP model, by shifting the focus from the stressor, you break the mental strategy involved in stressing yourself. For example, suppose to stress yourself you first see (visual) the stressing agent, then you say to yourself (auditory internal dialogue) "This is bad." Next you feel (kinaesthetic) bad and fearful and your brain tells your body including your immune system to prepare for danger. Next, adrenaline starts flowing, heart rate increases, blood leaves the brain and goes to the muscles for flight or fight, etc.

How did you stress yourself? You had a strategy that worked really well. You saw the stressor, you talked to yourself and you felt fear and the body did the rest. Now, what happens in the freeze frame model when you move your focus from the stressor to your heart? You have taken out the visual picture which served as the trigger for the strategy to run and caused you stress. Without the trigger, the strategy will not run and you cannot stress yourself. You have dissociated from that which stressed you.

Now, pretending your breathing comes from your heart also provides an ingenious way to induce a trance, which also helps to reduce stress. Obviously a person cannot breathe through the heart. To pretend one breathes from the heart provides an excellent example of a hypnotic language pattern from the medical hypnotherapy of Milton Erickson, MD.

If I said to you, "Your chair cries out to you to sit down and relax," I would utilise this pattern as I gave life to an inanimate object. Such ambiguous language induces a trance. A trance causes a switch in dominance in the brain stem of norepinephrine and acetylcholine2. Since a trance induces relaxation, utilising language, which induces trance, decreases stress and its symptoms.

Step 3

"Recall a positive fun feeling or time you've had in life and attempt to re-experience it."

Such language as this rings the bell of the NLP practitioner. NLP holds the firm conviction that to eliminate a problem you must find a resource capable enough to eliminate the problem. Following the teachings of Milton Erickson, each client has their own sufficient resources.

I refer you back to association/dissociation. In NLP we:

- dissociate the client from the problem,
- associate the client to the resources,
- associate resources to the problem and
- future pace resources to the future.

Here, in step 3, the author includes the all-important step of associating the client into the needed resources to overcome the stressor.

How do you re-experience a resource? By recalling a specific time when you had access to that needed resource that enabled you to feel "at your best". Imagine yourself now as if there – seeing through your eyes, hearing what you heard externally and internally and feeling what you felt. Associate yourself there now totally and completely and anchor in those feelings so you can recall them at will.

Obviously, this step also serves as a major disrupter of the stressing strategy.

Step 4

"Now, using your intuition, common sense and sincerity – ask your heart, what would be a more efficient response to the situation, one that will minimise future stress?"

Here the model deepens the trance and relaxation by utilising the linguistic pattern of a selectional restriction violation. "Ask your heart." "Gracious," the conscious mind goes, "nonsense!" The unconscious mind on the other hand seeks to make sense out of this ambiguity, and as it does, this induces a state of trance as the person has to go "inside" to try to make sense out of a "heart" talking.

Many in NLP utilise this same format when they describe problem behaviours as "unconscious parts".

Linguistically, a "talking heart" and a "talking unconscious part" both provide examples of a selectional restriction violation. In my opinion and from my observation, they both work beautifully.

Now, I would change the language just a little bit by adding some presuppositions like, "If your heart could speak, what would your heart have to say to you about the way you now react to this situation and how could you best react in the future that would provide you a behaviour with an outcome that would be far more congruent with all parts of you?"

Step 5

"Listen to what your heart says in answer to your question. (It is an effective way to put your reactive mind and emotions in check – and an 'in-house' source of common sense solutions!)"

Following up on step 4, this step continues the deepening of the trance and relaxation. These last two steps give the unconscious mind permission to instruct the individual in more appropriate behaviours in response to the stress.

To add to this, one could utilise the basic idea in NLP as explained in step 3. "As you now recall that positive feeling from step 3 and as you totally and completely experience that now, and also have access to the information your heart just gave you, taking both of these resources into the future stress when you would have formerly reacted in the old way, notice how you can now react having these added resources."

Such language patterns tend to associate the client into the resource of step 3. The language also associates the client into the resource of the message from the heart (steps 4 and 5). Then it will bring those resources associated into an imagined future problem state, which will cause the positive resources to lapse into the negative problem. If the resources come with enough strength, this will eliminate the problem and train the unconscious mind to react more positively to any future stressor.

8
Bringing More Health into Everyday Life

◆

In NLP, we primarily tap into the magic of transforming meaning by the process of reframing, writes L. Michael Hall, Ph.D. By this we refer to the process whereby we create or offer new, different and more enhancing frames-of-references. In doing so, we frame our thinking in new and different ways, we take a different point of view, we alter our perspective, or we entertain new thoughts. Given the basic holistic neurolinguistic principle, this transforms not only the way we think but also the way we somatically feel. Thus when we shift from thought viruses that make our body–mind toxic to thought vitamins we think–feel in ways that more holistically support life and wellbeing.

The basic neurolinguistic principle? We do not have "mind" and "body" as separate and disconnected elements, what we "think" (using a variety of representation modes) inevitably and inescapably affects our "feelings" (our neurological response to representation). This explains how reframing meaning has psychosomatic effects on our bodily health, whether for better or for worse.

Ways to reframe – let me count the ways

While numerous other models of human functioning utilise reframing (Brief psychotherapy, Solution-Focus, Narrative, Ericksonian, etc.), NLP provides six basic reframing directions – six directions for shifting consciousness creating different frames (content, counter, pre-framing, post-framing, deframing and outframing) with twenty specific patterns for reframing.

The meta-move of outframing

When we move to a meta-position ("go meta") and out-frame, we typically bring one state of mind-and-body to bear upon another lower-level state. In outframing we thus put a larger frame-of-reference around our belief or meaning, generating a larger-level context within which the old frame then operates. This is known as meta-stating (i.e. bringing one state of mind–body to bear upon another state).

Thus in accessing our thoughts and feelings about other thoughts and feelings, we reflect on the previous products of our consciousness. This activates our self-reflexive consciousness so that we "abstract" to a higher logical level, a level about a lower level. This puts us in a meta-state position – usually enabling us to adopt a more objective stance, sometimes as dissociative stance, but sometimes as stance that amplifies the lower state as in fear-about-fear or guilt-about-anger.

Meta-stating/outframing states of distress

In ill health, illness, disease and/or dysfunction we experience a primary state of distress. Here various cues (in the form of thoughts, images, sounds, sensations, words, etc.) signal our nervous systems (central and autonomic) as well as our immune system about illness.

Much of NLP to date has focused on exploring the question of how we represent (in our sensory modalities and sublimities) and the words that we use in coding and representing psychosomatic states of distress. For example, we might explore how we represent an allergy, headache, cold, etc. Doing this begins the process of identifying our strategy for a state of distress. "Hello, I'm from a temporary employment agency. If you teach me how to have this experience, you get a day off."

But now let's make a meta-move and look at the higher level thoughts-and-feelings that we may typically bring to bear on our states of distress that may make the state worse, and in fact begin a pathological process. How about the following?

"I hate to feel this way!"

"Why do I have to be this way? It's not fair!"

"I'll always be this way. Nothing ever works."

"Getting healthy is a matter of luck – the right doctor, the right medicine..."

"Some people just have healthier genes. They don't have the struggles that I do."

"I gain weight just by looking at food..."

"It's too much work to eat right, exercise regularly, etc."

When we take a meta-level position to an unpleasant primary state and bring a state of hate, rejection, non acceptance, a discounting state, an excuse-making/victim state to that – we outframe our distress state in a way that usually amplifies the distress. The state-about-a-state that then results generates a layered complexity and a gestalt of pain.

Such self-reflexivity can really create a life of living hell! How we communicate to ourselves about our primary states can initiate increased states of psycho-somatic distress. But we can take this internal mechanism of reflexivity and also use it for vitality and wellbeing. If, for example, we bring more empowering states to bear upon our distress, we can generate a more enhancing overall gestalt. Here we outframe our distress with more useful thoughts–feelings.

The subjective structure of many psycho-physiological states that ultimately result in sickness, disease, psycho-somatic problems arises because of the negative emotional (mental emotional) states (meta-states) that we have brought to bear upon some original difficulty. The problem doesn't merely lie in the fact that we have a headache – but that we hate our headache. The way we "run our brain" about our internal experiences can turn our psychic (mental–emotional) energies against ourselves to our detriment. We can thereby layer our experience so that we live in a meta-state of non-acceptance, self-rejection, self-hatred of our experiences.

Herein lies the paradox and ironic nature of accessing states of joy, pleasantness, acceptance, humour, imperfectionism (in contrast to perfectionism), affection, meaningfulness about our fallibilities, hurts, dysfunctions. As we lighten up and cease to take such primary states so seriously, we set a higher level frame-of-reference around things (outframe). This creates "magic" (neuro-semantic and neurolinguistic magic) at a higher level. Thus the seeming magic of accepting and welcoming my headache. Typically the headache vanishes.

The heart of a great many NLP and Ericksonian approaches to states of ill health involves outframing, at a higher logical level, a frame-of-reference of acceptance, love, purpose/meaning. In Milton Erickson's classic approach to headaches, he first simply accepts its presence and then encourages a welcoming of it by having a person curiously explore just what type of kinaesthetic qualities comprises it.

"Does it throb or pound? Do you feel pressure or heat?"

"Where do you centrally feel it? Where does it begin to fade out?"

"And if each throb is like a kitten stomping its feet – and you imagine the kitten stomping even harder..."

At a higher level Erickson presupposed that the person could become curious about the pain, and that by accepting it from the frame of curiosity about how much control one has over the submodality qualities, one's experience changes. Then "magic" begins to occur. It could happen.

9
A Journey to Total Health

◆

Did you know that we were created to live in total health, asks Neurolinguistic Programming psychologist John Tozeland. That is our natural state! In fact we have a blueprint for perfect health in our consciousness. Yet most of us experience states of disease from time to time, and some of us constantly live in a state of ill health. How can that be? Some traditions say that we have a river of energy flowing through our bodies, a series of streams and rivers that when in their natural state, flow freely through our body. When those rivers are clear, we are in a state of love, joy and happiness. Our life is easy and we have energy to spare.

With the passage of time our river system becomes polluted. Polluted by our thoughts, our emotions, our beliefs, the food we eat, etc. Log jams form, causing the water to back up and overflow the banks. In time the overflow creates new channels, and a new pattern or habit is formed. The goal of emotional, physical and spiritual growth is to clear out the pollution, take down the log jams and restore the old pathways and rivers, Tozeland says.

According to Dr Paul Goodwin from Alaska State University, when emotions and limiting beliefs are locked in our bodies there is actually a functional boundary formed around it. This boundary effectively blocks the flow of energy. As messages are sent in our bodies, they run into these blocks and are deflected somewhere else in the body. Needless to say this causes disease, as energy does not reach the point it is heading for.

In the modern world we are taught to compartmentalise ourselves. We are taught to "grin and bear it", to "endure" pain, etc. We tend to think that we are only a conscious mind and emphasise our willpower. We prevent ourselves from experiencing our emotions by continually denying them. Traditions like Huna and Midewin teach us that we have three selves: our conscious mind which is our willpower; our unconscious mind, which is the domain of our emotions and beliefs; and our higher self which is our perfection, our god selves. In our culture, we are generally taught that all we are is a conscious mind, yet it is this belief that prevents us from enjoying total health. We alienate ourselves from our inner selves, a part of us that is our best friend, a part of us that knows how to create perfect health, a part of us that respects us so much that it will not interfere until asked. As long as this alienation persists, we are prevented from having total health.

The greatest gift that you can be given is to be introduced to this "inner you". Once the communication is opened up, transformation begins. Sometimes this connection is made through meditation, sometimes through prayer, sometimes through hypnosis, sometimes through bodywork, etc. Once this connection is made the unconscious mind is ready to clear out the log jams so the energy can flow freely once more. When the unconscious mind is clear, we can then connect once more with our higher selves, our perfection. Alternate or complementary therapies, to be effective, Tozeland believes, must address the deeper parts of the individual to work with the cause of the disease, not just the symptoms.

Dr Henri Marcoux, a Network Chiropractor in Winnipeg, writes "...to be who you are, your nervous system must be clear of who you are not. By greater contact of your 'educated mind' (conscious mind) with your 'infinite consciousness' (unconscious mind and higher self) you are transformed. Planetary healing begins with personal healing."

10
What Causes Disease?

◆

According to Chinese pathology, researcher Anna Selby writes, there are three principal causes of the disharmony that brings about disease: external factors, emotions and irregularities in day-to-day living.

External causes

External causes embrace a range of environmental conditions: wind, cold, fire, dryness, dampness and summer heat. Wind causes movement and change. It invades the body and causes dizziness, twitching, stiffness and convulsions. When combined with cold, it engenders colds, chills, flu and fever. It is related to the liver and can cause epilepsy and stroke. Its effects are thought to be strongest in the spring. Cold constrains movement and warmth, often leading to stagnation. As well as possibly causing colds and chills when combined with wind, it can affect the lungs, resulting in expectorated mucus, and also affect the stomach and spleen, leading to vomiting or diarrhoea. Fire dries and its associated ailments include fevers, inflammations, constipation and infrequent urination. Psychologically, it results in irritability, lack of concentration, delirium and manic behaviour. In children it can sometimes result in hyperactivity. Dryness has a similar action to fire but with a tendency to dry body fluids. Symptoms include dry skin, cracked lips, a persistent cough with no phlegm and constipation. Dampness brings feelings of heaviness and sluggishness. Typical symptoms include headaches, lethargy, bloating, nausea and stiff, swollen and aching joints. Summer heat causes sunstroke, exhaustion and dehydration. It can result in fever and nausea.

Internal causes

The importance of a balanced state extends to the emotions and mind as well as the body. An excess or a lack of emotional expression can lead to disharmony that will manifest itself in both emotional and physical symptoms. No particular emotion is regarded as good or bad – any imbalance is seen as a potential cause of illness.

Joy in excess leads to over-excitement or agitation, injury to the heart, insomnia, palpitation and hysteria. Anger causes resentment, frustration, rage and bitterness, injury to the liver, headaches, high blood pressure, menstrual problems and ailments of the stomach or spleen. Sadness affects the lungs and the heart and also causes breathlessness, fatigue, lowered immunity and insomnia. Pensiveness is caused by mental overwork or intellectual over-stimulation and may lead to obsessiveness. It affects the spleen and also causes poor concentration, lethargy, loss of appetite and anaemia. Fear affects the kidneys, causing incontinence in adults and bed-wetting in children. It also reduces fertility, libido and general immunity to infection. Shock affects the kidneys and the heart. Imbalances also lead to palpitation, insomnia and fatigue.

Lifestyle causes

The Chinese desire for balance in all things naturally includes the way we live our lives. Again, excesses or deficits are seen as generators of disease. Diet is very important in traditional Chinese medicine. A good diet is the foundation of good health and many ailments are cured simply by addressing basic nutritional imbalances. The ideal Chinese diet comprises food which is slightly warm to slightly cool in energy, such as fish, chicken, pork, beef, grains, cooked vegetables and certain fruits. Certain hot foods, especially fried foods, and drinks such as coffee, tea, chocolate, as well as cold foods, including salads and frozen foods like ice cream, should be taken in very limited amounts. Salt, sugar, caffeine and alcohol are regarded as toxins.

Exercise supports the flow of energy. Without it, the Qi will stagnate. Excessive exercise, however, will lead to lowered immunity. In Chinese terms, exercise takes the form of techniques such as Tai Chi and Qi Gong (pronounced chi kung), which focus on balance and concentration, the movements of the body being informed by both mind and spirit. Energetic exercise, for example aerobic exercise, has no role to play in the Chinese philosophy. Excessive libido and repeated childbirth can damage the health by sapping Qi energy. These can also result in lower back pain and failing hearing and eyesight.

Patterns of disharmony

Disharmony may be caused by external and internal factors or the excesses and deficiencies of an unbalanced lifestyle. Depending on the nature of the root cause, a pattern of disharmony is set up within the body and mind. It is the diagnosis of this underlying pattern that is the basis of the Chinese physician's treatment. There are numerous patterns of disharmony, many of which overlap, but most Chinese herbalists work from approximately seventy-five patterns, with innumerable further variations on these. The patterns themselves rest upon the Eight Principles: yin and yang, interior and exterior, cold and heat, deficiency and excess.

Yin and yang make up the basic guiding principle for diagnosis. Yang embraces the exterior, heat and symptoms and conditions related to excess. Yin embraces the interior, cold and symptoms and conditions related to deficiency. There are four potent imbalances: yang excess exhibits itself in fever, impatience, bad temper, headaches, rapid pulse and high blood pressure. Yang deficiency often shows itself in night sweats, exhaustion, constipation, backache and impotence. Yin excess, which is very rarely seen, manifests itself in lethargy, aches, shivering, fluid retention and excessive mucus occurring in the lungs and nasal passages, in the bowel and as a vaginal discharge. Yin deficiency is exhibited in nervous exhaustion and tension, hot flushes and fevers.

The words "interior" and "exterior" refer to the location of the ailment. Exterior conditions are caused by external factors and affect the skin, nose, mouth and hair. Symptoms include colds and fevers, injuries, sweating and skin problems. They are usually mild and often relieved by inducing sweating. Interior conditions are more severe and are usually caused by emotional and lifestyle factors. There is a range of symptoms, depending on the organ affected, including constipation, diabetes, infertility, impotence, lowered energy and heart problems. Treatment depends upon which organ is affected.

11
Importance of Good Nutrition

◆

It is important to become aware of the effect on the body of what we eat, and how foods affect how we feel, writes Catherine Sutton, author of *Discover Shiatsu*. The most beneficial change is to cut out "extreme foods", foods that seem to have the most dramatic effect on the body. These often are, unfortunately, eaten in large quantities. The extreme effect of such foods is no longer acknowledged by the body since it becomes an accepted way of feeding for many people. An example is that of drinking strong coffee. This creates a stress-like response in the body – shaking hands, heart palpitation, dilated pupils, poor digestion and sweating. These symptoms are often accepted as "normal", because they are continuously present in some people to a greater or lesser degree.

These symptoms may be a background discomfort that can be tolerated, but stimulants create a strain on the body. It is not healthy to have a system that is constantly on the alert and under stress. By taking regular stimulants such as caffeine, sugar, alcohol, drugs and cigarettes the body cannot relax properly. This can be a contributory factor in many stress-related disorders such as ulcers, migraines, irritable bowel syndrome, psoriasis and asthma. Too many stimulants alter the mind state, thus preventing real clarity.

There are also foods that have the opposite effect, that of depressing the system. These are mainly animal foods, particularly red meat, heavy dairy foods (butter, cheese, mayonnaise, ice cream, cream) and salt. They appear to slow down the digestive system, taking a long time to pass through it. This sluggishness gives rise to constipation, bowel disorders, and other symptoms such as acne, low energy, low motivation and depression. A lot of red meat slows down the body and mind. Dairy foods are also often a contributory factor in the build-up of mucus in the body, particularly in the respiratory tract, the sinuses, the ears and the female reproductive organs.

In most spiritual disciplines originating from the East, there is little emphasis on animal foods, with a tendency towards vegetarianism instead. Basic recommendations for a more balanced and nutritious diet are as follows:

Foods to cut down:
    red meat
    dairy foods
    sugar/biscuits/cakes
    oils (except olive oil)
    tea, coffee and alcohol
    refined foods.

Foods to increase:
    vegetable protein (lentils, beans and nuts)
    whole grains (brown rice, barley, millet, oats)
    fresh vegetables
    fresh fruits
    home-made soups
    soy-based products.

When some dietary changes are made there can be a reaction in the body that may seem negative. If caffeine has been taken in large quantities over a number of years, the body will experience withdrawal symptoms such as headaches and nausea. These will pass within a couple of days – be patient! If you have been used to eating a lot of animal products and then either cut them down or give them up, you may get symptoms of detoxification. Your skin may temporarily become blotchy or spotty and you may feel tired. It is worth persevering.

If you give up animal food altogether, you will have to find your protein from vegetable sources such as beans, lentils, nuts and seeds. Soybean products are a fine way to get protein and include soy milk, soy sausages and burgers. You may wish just to cut down consumption of red meat to start with and still eat chicken and fish. Take care not to overdose on chicken unless it is free range; there can be toxic residues in it. Fish is a good source of fatty acids, calcium and protein. To give up all sugar can be very difficult because there are hidden sugars in so many refined products – even salty ones. Beware of foods that say they are sugar free; their manufacturers often have a different way of presenting sugar, such as sucrose, maltose or dextrose. Some people think that honey is a good substitute, but it contains a high percentage of different forms of sugar.

Eat in moderation and chew your food well. Try not to eat when stressed. If you are anxious about something, take a few long slow breaths before you start your meal. If you do this, you will eat in a more relaxed way and your digestive system will function better. See how much of your eating is done consciously and how much is done mindlessly, anxiously and out of a need for comfort. Food should be used to nourish the physical body, not as an emotional crutch.

12
Nutritional Therapy

Nutritional therapy, says researcher Patricia Quinn, is a system of healing based on the belief that food, as nature intended, provides the medicine we need to obtain and maintain a state of health: our food is our medicine and our medicine is our food.

Although some health problems require specific medication, many conditions can be relieved effectively with nutritional therapy. These include disorders ranging from chronic fatigue, energy loss, insomnia and depression to backache, skin complaints, asthma and headaches. Nutritional therapy will also benefit you if you have no specific illness but want to maintain a state of optimum health. It is safe for babies and children as well as for adults, and the change of eating patterns that is typically prescribed usually has far fewer side-effects than synthetic medicines, Quinn advises.

Nutritional therapy is a holistic discipline; nutrition as the key to good health is the all-embracing fundamental principle used since the time of the famous Greek doctor and founder of Western medicine, Hippocrates, to help people of all ages to stay at their personal peak of energy and vitality. Today, new insights of food scientists play a significant role in the practice of nutritional therapy as preventative medicine.

During the last fifty years, many wonderful breakthroughs have improved our understanding of the role of food in our lives. But at the same time, many of us are realising that food is the cornerstone which, in our modern lifestyle, has been rejected by the builder, says Quinn.

The speed at which we live and work – the pressure of the deadline – pushes us into a fast-eating culture, where quality of food becomes secondary. Eating on the job, on the run, under pressure, denies us the experience, the purpose and the role of food. Eventually it denies us our very lifestyle. Modern supermarkets are stocked with many instant meals, but more often than not these meals are far lower in nutritional value than those prepared at home with fresh organically grown ingredients. For all the benefits agribusiness has brought the people of the Western world, the disadvantages of the modern food industry include extensive use of chemicals in food production. There is also a loss of the vitality intrinsic in newly harvested food because many products are transported vast distances before they reach their destination. Of course, this is the case with many of the so-called "fresh" foods on our supermarket shelves, as well as with those dishes that have been pre-cooked and packaged before reaching the supermarkets, according to Quinn.

Lifestyle and nutrition are intimately linked and our lifestyle defines itself partly from the tradition of the country we live in and partly from our attitudes. How do you really want to live? Given the choice, would you prefer to eat well every day, to exercise, to breathe clean air as often as possible, to drink a reasonable amount of water in order to keep your bloodstream clean and able to wash out toxins? This choice is available to all of us, but to exercise it we need to understand the impact on our wellbeing of different foods and learn from direct experience what kind of eating pattern best suits our lifestyle, Quinn maintains.

What is health?

In a dynamic and good state of health, our mental, emotional, physical and spiritual components all live in harmony with each other. For a wider comprehension of health, it is interesting to look at the issue of "healthiness" not only from the Western but also from the Eastern point of view. The ancient systems of Chinese and Indian medicine go back more than 5,000 years. These cultures used – and continue to use – whole plants in their treatment, whereas modern medicine uses extracts from plants, which are often then replicated by synthetic products.

The two systems of medicine diverge at the point of prevention. Eastern practices include the preventative care of the whole person as a primary aim – to maintain good health. The formula for good health is:

- life force
- good-quality blood
- proper nourishment.

Our daily diet will make good-quality blood, which in turn promotes the flow of healthy energy. We need to daily ask ourselves questions like, What is my physical health like today? Do I have a sense of wellbeing? Do I have plenty of energy? Do I sleep and eat well? How we feel each day is built upon our past actions, our past dietary practices, whether we have had physical exercise, whether we have been mentally active, and on our general attitude towards life.

Tiredness versus fatigue

Fatigue is very prevalent in the present day. The healthy person who uses his or her entire body in the ways described above during each day will feel tired – the pleasant feeling of having worked hard. This individual's body will be able to relax completely and recuperate at the end of the day. This is not fatigue – it is the body's natural need for rest. It is during rest and recuperation that the body cleanses itself of all the toxins that build up during activity. If the body is not given a chance to self-cleanse, a state of fatigue will become persistent. When it becomes chronic, fatigue may indicate underlying problems, such as infection, immune system weaknesses, glandular problems or lymphatic congestion, as the body's systems become clogged by waste, according to Quinn.

What is illness?

Illness develops in four stages:
- tiredness, changing to fatigue – no amount of rest seems adequate
- irritability
- symptoms
- illness.

The Eastern approach to health divides the causes of illness into two: those that come from within and those that come from without. Those from within are mostly products of our lifestyle, traditions and beliefs. The ways we can be affected from within are as follows:
- excess of emotions, even positive ones such as joy, can affect the heart
- excess of anger can affect the liver
- excess of sadness damages the appetite, the stomach, spleen or pancreas
- excessive grief can affect the lungs
- shock, fear, surprise, or fright can affect the kidneys.

Part of the process of nutritional therapy is to help us

restore the proper balance, to bring about the harmony we lack.

The "four doctors"

The basic needs of our physical bodies to eliminate toxic waste as described above, Quinn maintains, are being denied to us by the life we lead in modern Western society. What we require to attend to these basic needs Quinn calls the "four doctors":

1. sunlight and fresh air
2. proper exercise and sufficient rest
3. good food
4. pure water.

While our ancestors lived mainly outdoor lives, we tend to live largely indoors, denying ourselves the most pivotal requirement: light. Our whole body depends on the reception of light in order to carry out vital functions – the regulation of the appetite, our patterns of sleeping and waking, aspects of our behaviour and the health of our nervous system.

Fresh air is necessary for us to exchange the toxins and pollutants in the body with at least an equal amount of air, otherwise, we develop acute respiratory problems from overload. Our cities do not have sufficient trees to breathe back oxygen into our environment. Trees act as "lungs" by filling the air with life-giving oxygen.

Water is the greatest treat for the body. It is the river that carries all the nutrients around the body to the brain and to every single cell in the body. The brain is the first place to suffer dehydration – it then becomes difficult to think or make appropriate decisions. In recent studies, it was found that water more than food helped give long-distance walkers the energy to finish. Likewise, those driving long distances need a snack, as well as a break of fifteen minutes or so, in order to maintain their concentration on the road. In both of these examples, the simple remedies prevented emotional and psychological imbalance, which drains the body of its energy supply and causes fatigue.

The role of food in our lives

By experimenting with the effects of different foods, many people find they also revise old beliefs about the role of food in their lives. Nutritional therapy is not just about eating different types of food – it is also about increasing your awareness of how you eat and of where the food you eat comes from, of how you store and prepare it, and of how you perceive yourself and your place in the web of life. The benefits of nutritional therapy are sometimes immediate, but its study is timeless and its effects can bring about long-lasting changes in your attitude to life.

Dr Henry Dreher, author of *The Immune Power Personality*, reminds us of certain characteristics we can all develop which increase our ability to be healthy. These characteristics include:
- having the ability to recognise when the body is signalling to us that it is in pain or feeling tired
- identifying emotions such as anger or sadness
- connecting these states to food we have recently eaten and so learning to identify the effects different foods have on us
- developing a sense of control over our health and over the quality of our lives, because the way we live – as well as the way we eat – is part of the way we nourish ourselves.

Nutritional therapy helps us consider our human immunity in the context of a rapidly changing environment by deepening our understanding of the constant ebb and flow between ourselves and our outer world. Our immunity is part of the entire picture – a relationship between our own evolving and our world. "Whole body" immunity concerns all aspects of life: ensuring that the physical body has the correct nutrition and appropriate healing therapies, enjoying good emotional health by nurturing the feelings, learning to make choices from a position of unbiased awareness and not from the "victim" or "martyr" approach.

Nutritional therapy requires us to acknowledge that we are body, soul, mind and emotion. Accordingly, it incorporates all these aspects of our lives, with the objective of maintaining a healthy mind and soul as well as a healthy body, developing an open-minded outlook and a positive attitude to ourselves, and learning to see any causes of stress in our lives as challenges rather than threats, Quinn concludes.

13
Eat According to Your Blood Group

———◆———

You are what you eat, say Steven M. Weissberg, MD, and Joseph Christiano, APPT, but you should "*Eat what you are.*" This means each of us should eat the optimal diet compatible with our blood type. Doing this sounds easy enough, but in practice it is much harder to achieve. For example, in the animal kingdom instinct is what drives animals to eat. Lions are meat eaters. Try and feed a lion carbohydrates such as fruits and vegetables and you already know the result. Conversely, other animals are vegetarian, and by instinct will not eat meat. This is no accident. Instinct is a protective mechanism for all animals, including humans. The problem is humans are so domesticated, instinct no longer drives their eating habits. What we can learn from animals is they eat only what is instinctively good for them, and as a result heart disease is virtually non-existent among them. While animals occasionally do develop cancer, statistically it occurs dramatically less often than in humans.

Additionally, have you ever noticed most animals of a given species all live to about the same age? Well, this is because of their uniform diets, driven by instinct, that allow them to have life spans to the potential of their species. Another point to remember is most animals that are not killed by predators die of old age, or what we call natural causes.

With humans it is just the opposite, the only exception being the many people of blood type O who die of old age. Humans almost always die from one disease or another. As a result of our improper diets, our immune systems fail to operate properly and we become susceptible to one disease or another. Medical science has come a long way and has prolonged life for many. But as Ben Franklin once said, "An ounce of prevention is worth a pound of cure." These words of wisdom are still true today.

We have the ability to treat illness and operate when necessary. But in many cases, much of what modern medicine does is treat the symptom or outward manifestation of the problem, not prevent the problem in the first place. It is not for us to place blame, as medicine is providing many wonderful cures, vaccines and medications which are allowing people all over the world to live longer, more productive lives. However, we believe the emphasis currently is on the treatment, when it should be on the prevention.

It all starts in our childhood. We grow up in families where we are given food our mothers and fathers believe is good for us, or tastes good. The fact that it tastes good is not an indication of whether the food is good for us. Our blood types were determined at the moment of conception and although we may be able to change almost everything about ourselves, we cannot change our blood types. Each blood type has different characteristics that allow it to eat, digest and assimilate food best for that group. Since Os have been blessed with such strong stomach acid and respective enzymes, they are able to metabolise almost everything, even those foods not recommended for them. However, the Bs, As and ABs do not have this luxury, and accordingly must be more careful in their eating habits, or suffer the consequences.

The Os are like sharks. They can eat tin cans and rubber tyres, and wash them down with hard liquor while smoking a cigarette! Of course, this is not true – just a dramatic exaggeration! Nevertheless, Type Os have the highest threshold for abuse of any blood group, and in the final analysis it is another reason they live longer.

Now let's get back to our eating habits and what happens when we eat food not compatible with our blood enzymes and stomach acid. Agglutination takes place. What's that, you ask? Well, we humans have a process being effected in our blood called agglutination. Let me explain. Your body has antibodies that protect it from foreign invaders. Your immune system produces all kinds of antibodies to protect you and keep you safe from foreign substances. Each antibody is designed to attach itself to a foreign substance or antigen.

When your body recognises an intruder, it produces more antibodies to attack the invader. The antibody then attaches itself to the intruder and a "gluing" effect takes place. In this way the body can better dispose of these foreign invaders.

For example, if you eat a food not compatible with your blood type and stomach enzymes, the food is not broken down or digested properly, and the vitamins and minerals are not absorbed into your bloodstream to fuel and nourish your body. Your body reacts to the food just as it would to any foreign substance. You might experience a stomach ache, gas, bloating or, even worse, vomiting or diarrhoea. What happens is that antibodies glue themselves to the foreign invaders (improper food) and agglutination or "gluing" takes place in your blood.

Now if you happen to be blood type A, who already has thick blood, your blood becomes even thicker. The thicker the blood, the slower it moves and the harder your heart must pump to push the blood through your arteries. This thick slow-moving blood makes it easier for plaque to build up on your artery walls. Hence, high blood pressure, heart disease or a cornucopia of other illnesses. You get the picture.

The human body is a wonderful and complex

organism. It tries to handle everything you give it, but sometimes it cannot, or will not. The damage is greater or lesser, depending on how bad the food is for you and your particular body chemistry. If you are lucky, maybe this improper agglutination may result only in weight gain. The body does not use the food, so it just packs on extra pounds. You are not eating much, but you're gaining weight and don't know why. Well, the answer is improper metabolism of your food.

If you are Type A or AB and the meat you keep eating is not metabolising, your bloodstream is now flooded with thick, sticky agglutinated blood, loaded with saturated animal fat, just looking for a nice spot to deposit itself. It doesn't take a genius IQ to see why As and ABs should not eat meat, and if they do, they die younger.

Now if Os or Bs eat meat, their bodies metabolise it better and the agglutination process does not take place, or if it does, it is very minor and not life threatening. Type Os, who usually completely metabolise meat and gain all the benefits from it (with the exception of pork) are at little or no risk. Further, since an O starts out with the thinnest blood, any agglutination that takes place will thicken the blood, but not to the extent experienced by the other blood types, or to the point of being life threatening.

Take, for example, bread and white potatoes. If a Type O or Type A eats these foods, in most cases some agglutination takes place. However, since these foods contain little, if any, fat, the body will not deposit the non-metabolised portion on the artery walls. It is more likely to store the unused food as fat. Hence, you gain weight. While this may be benevolent in the short run, eventually all this excess fat may lead to diabetes, high blood pressure or other illnesses.

Any food containing saturated fat has the greatest

potential for doing harm to the body in the long run, regardless of blood type. Saturated fat to Types A and AB is more dangerous in the short run because of the reasons stated previously. In the long run, even Types O and B, whose blood enzymes handle saturated fat better, are susceptible to the hazards. It just takes longer. So although Os and Bs are not particularly susceptible to heart disease and most forms of cancer, a continual regimen of saturated fat and/or incompatible foods will eventually produce the same result. It just appears the harmful effects take much longer to show in Os and Bs.

Saturated fats in the diet in any form will eventually undermine your health. Of the saturated fats, the most damaging come from animal protein. To eliminate this risk, acquire much of your protein, regardless of blood type, from sources that are fat free, or free of animal saturated fat.

In the final analysis, most of what needs to take place so as to enable us to avoid disease, boost the immune function and maintain weight control – in short, to achieve the best results for your body – is all based on diet. To succeed requires balancing proteins, carbohydrates and fats in the proportions best for your body.

As the body grows older, it stops producing certain hormones, it loses muscle mass, bones become more brittle, immune function decreases and the body's intolerance of improper food begins to manifest itself in insidious ways.

But with proper diet, including nourishment from those foods and supplements specific to your needs, the chance of disease is greatly reduced. In fact, proper diet according to blood type, coupled with exercise, enables your immune system to be its strongest. A strong immune system can make the difference between a longer or shorter life span.

14
How to Calm the Mind with Touch

◆

Stress reduction methods

The term "relaxation response" was coined by Dr Herbert Benson, who wrote a book by that name. All stress-reduction techniques generate this response, marked by physical and mental features which contribute to good health. These include a decrease in oxygen consumption, blood pressure, muscle tension, breathing and heart beat. Brainwave patterns are also altered to elicit a state we commonly think of as "peace of mind", during which we can let go of worries and distracting thoughts: the brainwaves known as "alpha" become dominant.

Dr Benson distils four components common to all stress-reduction techniques: a quiet environment; a comfortable position; a passive attitude (letting it happen rather than trying to make it happen); and a mental device. He describes mental device as "a sound, word, or phrase repeated silently or aloud; or fixed gazing at an object".

Using touch instead of a mental device according to Eliott Cherry, BA, LMT, NCTMB, is more effective. Mental techniques which may seem difficult or time-consuming to study can dissuade many people from learning a stress-reduction method. The mind may seem hard to control at times, but he has found that touch automatically and effortlessly focuses the mind, allowing it to let go of unwanted thoughts. No meditation experience is required.

Why touch works

There are many reasons why using the sense of touch works particularly well as a method and structure for focus and relaxation. You are probably aware of many anecdotes about the animal kingdom and the power of touch. There are the tales of lizards, frogs, dogs, cats and horses who seem to go into a meditative state when stroked. Cherry says he had the pleasure of meeting a pot-bellied pig, named Dolly Bacon, who simply collapsed when he rubbed her belly! And what about the person receiving a massage? For many of us, being stroked, or a simple hug, is enough to send troublesome thoughts out of our minds and tension out of our bodies.

When we are active in touching, rather than being the passive recipient of touch, we are still stimulating our touch receptors; we are indeed still being touched. This may be why a person's blood pressure is lowered when petting a dog or cat and why many massage therapists report feeling more relaxed after giving a massage, regardless of the physical work involved. In speaking of touch, it is interesting to look at the properties of skin. It is our largest organ, our protector and our most pervasive contact with the environment. The skin as a whole contains over 600,000 touch receptors. Both the skin and brain originate from the same cells and our sense of touch develops before hearing and sight. In fact, scientists have found that embryos less than eight weeks old already possess the sense of touch. Touch is our most discriminating sense. Woodworkers, for example, know they must feel to correct imperfections in their work which they cannot see.

It is no wonder that touch – particularly a stroking motion – is a powerful tool for concentration. Our attention is predisposed to automatically remain fixed on the object stroked, so much so that our minds are filled with the stimulus. There is no need to try and control the mind to keep it from wandering away from a mental device such as a repeated phrase. There is also no need to attempt to keep the mind clear of distracting thoughts, a process often required when focusing on a visual object.

Children and touch

Many agree that children should develop relaxation and concentration skills as early as possible. This is particularly important for those living with Attention Deficit Disorder (ADD/ADHD). Because children love to touch, it is a naturally appealing way for them to learn these skills. Since there is no need to explain concepts or teach a mental discipline, children of varying ages and circumstances can relate easily to this method.

Improving focus and confidence

Over time, the regular practice of relaxed focus leads automatically to an improved ability to concentrate. By utilising this combination of focus and relaxation before and during challenging events, one can feel a greater sense of mastery. We can experience a pleasant chain reaction.

Gentle focus – relaxation – confidence

In fact, conscious relaxation techniques alone have been shown to lead to a greater sense of confidence. Musicians and athletes who must perform under pressure have observed this phenomenon.

Touch has particular appeal and usefulness before or during stressful events. Do we not associate fidgeting with nervousness? Touch allows us to channel this physical energy into a calming motion.

A demonstration

Find a quiet place to sit or lie down. Are your legs crossed? If so, uncross them. If they were not at first, cross them now. This helps to prepare your mind for something new. Let either hand rest on any convenient and comfortable surface. Take a deep breath, gently hold it for a few seconds, then exhale and let your eyes close. Now, allow any finger or combination of fingers to begin to stroke the surface. Allow your mind to enter your fingertips, almost as if you were living inside of them. Now pay attention to everything your fingertips feel. Use different parts of your fingertips, letting them move by themselves, tracing imaginary patterns. Notice any textures and the different curving motions of your hand and fingers. As you let yourself breathe deeply, slowly and comfortably, notice every subtle variation and continue as long as you wish. If appropriate, you can let yourself drift off to sleep. Otherwise, when you are ready to finish, take a deep breath, exhale, open your eyes and connect with your surroundings. Shake your arms and hands and move your body about so that you feel fully awake and alert.

Practise at home, then use this method during travel, before public speaking, tests or difficult meetings. Use it during work breaks and before bed. Share it with your children. Touch is powerful. Use it to your best advantage!

15
Therapeutic Touch

◆

"Various esoteric sources have long suggested that human beings are capable of healing one another by utilising the special energy potentials which are brought into each lifetime," writes Dr Richard Gerber, MD. This healing ability has had many names through the centuries, including laying on of hands healing, psychic healing, spiritual healing and therapeutic touch. Only in the last several decades has modern technology and the consciousness of enlightened scientists evolved to the point where laboratory confirmation of subtle energetic healing has been made possible.

Historical look at psychic healing

The use of laying on of hands to heal human illness dates back thousands of years in human history. Evidence for its use in ancient Egypt is found in the Ebers Papyrus dated at about 1552 BC. This document describes the use of laying on of hands healing for medical treatment. Four centuries before the birth of Christ, the Greeks used therapeutic touch therapy in their Asklepian temples for healing the sick. The writings of Aristophanes detail the use of laying on of hands in Athens to restore a blind man's sight and return fertility to a barren woman.

The Bible has many references to the laying on of hands for both medical and spiritual applications. It is well known that many of the miraculous healings of

Jesus were done by the laying on of hands. Jesus said, "These things that I do, so can you do and more." Laying on of hands healing was considered part of the work of the early Christian ministry as much as preaching and administering the sacraments. In the early Christian Church, laying on of hands was combined with the sacramental use of holy water and oil.

Over the hundreds of years that followed, the healing ministry of the Church began to gradually decline. In Europe the healing ministry was carried on as the royal touch. Kings of several European countries were purportedly successful in curing diseases such as tuberculosis (scrofula) by laying on of hands. In England, this method of healing began with Edward the Confessor, lasted for seven centuries and ended with the reign of the sceptical William IV. Many of the early attempts at laying on of hands healing seemed to be predicated upon a belief either in the powers of Jesus, or the king, or a particular healer. There were other contemporary medical theorists who felt that special vital forces and influences in nature were the mediators of these healing effects.

A number of early researchers into the mechanisms of healing theorised on the likely magnetic nature of the energies involved. One of the earliest proponents of a magnetic vital force of nature was the controversial physician Theophrastus Bombastus von Hohenheim, otherwise known as Paracelsus (1493–1541). In addition to his discoveries of new drug therapies, Paracelsus founded the sympathetic system of medicine, according to which the stars and other bodies (especially magnets) influenced humans by means of a subtle emanation or fluid that pervaded all space. His theory was an attempt to explain the apparent link between human beings and the stars and other heavenly bodies. Paracelsus' sympathetic system may be viewed as an early astrological belief about the influences of the planets and stars on human illness and behaviour. The proposed link between humans and the heavens above was through a subtle pervasive fluid, perhaps an early construct of the "ether", which existed throughout the universe. He attributed magnetic qualities to this subtle substance and felt that it possessed unique qualities of healing. He also concluded that if this force was possessed or wielded by someone, then that person could arrest or heal diseases in others. Paracelsus stated that the vital force was not enclosed inside an individual but radiated within and around them like a luminous sphere which could be made to act at a distance.

In the century following Paracelsus' death, the magnetic tradition was carried on by Robert Fludd, a physician and a mystic. Fludd was considered to be one of the most prominent alchemists of the early seventeenth century. He emphasised the role of the sun in health as a source of light and life. The sun was considered the purveyor of life beams required for all living creatures on earth. Fludd felt that this supercelestial and invisible force in some way manifested in all living things and that it entered the body through the breath. One is reminded of the Indian concept of prana, the subtle energy within sunlight which is assimilated through the process of breathing. Many esotericists feel that by mentally directing the visualised stream of inhaled prana, healers may focus this etheric energy through their hands and into the patient. Fludd also believed that the human being possessed the qualities of a magnet. In 1778 a radical healer stepped forward to say that he could achieve remarkable therapeutic success without the need for patients' faith in the healing powers of Jesus or himself. Franz Anton Mesmer claimed that the healing results which he obtained came through the enlightened use of a universal energy which he called fluidum. (There is an interesting similarity between the terminology of Mesmer's fluidum and the ethereal fluidum mentioned in Ryerson's channelled material, i.e. the substance of the etheric body.) Mesmer claimed that fluidum was a subtle physical fluid that filled the universe and was the connecting medium between people and other living things and between living organisms, the earth and the heavenly bodies. (This theory is quite similar to Paracelsus' concept of sympathetic medicine.) Mesmer suggested that all things in nature possessed a particular power which manifested itself through special actions upon other bodies. He felt that all physical bodies, animals, plants and even stones were impregnated with this magical fluid. During his early medical research in Vienna, Mesmer discovered that placing a magnet over areas of the body afflicted with disease would often effect a cure. Experiments with patients who had nervous disorders often produced unusual motor effects. Mesmer noted that successful magnetic treatments frequently induced pronounced muscle spasms and jerks. He came to believe that the magnets he used for therapy were mainly conductors of an ethereal fluid which issued forth from his own body to create subtle healing effects in patients. He considered this vital force or fluid to be of a magnetic nature, referring to it as "animal magnetism" (to distinguish it from mineral or ferromagnetism).

Through his research, Mesmer came to believe that this subtle energetic fluid was somehow associated with the nervous system, especially when his treatments would often cause involuntary muscle spasms and tremors. He hypothesised that the nerve and body fluids conveyed the fluid to all areas of the body, where it animated and revitalised those parts. Mesmer's concept of fluidum is reminiscent of the ancient Chinese theory of Qi energy which flows through the meridians, feeding the vital force to the nerves and tissues of the body.

Mesmer realised that the life-sustaining and regulating actions of the magnetic fluidum were integral to the basic processes of homeostasis and health. When the individual was in a state of health, he or she was considered to be in harmony with these most basic laws of nature, as expressed by a proper interplay of the vital magnetic forces. If disharmony occurred between the physical body and these subtle forces of nature, sickness was the end result. Mesmer later realised that the best source of this universal force was the human body itself. He felt that the most active points of energetic flow were from the palms of the hands. By placing the practitioner's hands on patients for direct healing, energy was allowed a direct route to flow from healer to patient. Because of Mesmer's influence during this revolutionary period in French history, the technique of laying on of hands, otherwise known as "magnetic passes", became quite popular.

Unfortunately, many scientific observers at the time considered mesmerism to be merely an act of hypnosis and suggestion. (To this day, many scientists still refer to hypnosis as mesmerism, thus the origin of the term mesmerised.)

In 1784, the king of France appointed a commission of inquiry into the validity of Mesmer's experiments in healing. Among the commission were members of the Academy of Sciences, the Academy of Medicine, the Royal Society, as well as the American statesman–scientist Benjamin Franklin. The experiments which they devised were constructed to test the presence or absence of the magnetic fluidum which Mesmer claimed was the healing force behind his therapeutic successes. Unfortunately, none of the tests devised by the commission were concerned with the measurement of fluidum's medical effects.

The conclusion of this prestigious commission was that fluidum did not exist. Although they did not deny Mesmer's therapeutic successes with patients, they felt that the medical effects which Mesmer produced were due to sensitive excitement, imagination and imitation (of other patients). Interestingly, a committee of the Medical Section of the Academie des Sciences examined animal magnetism again in 1831 and accepted Mesmer's viewpoint. However, despite this validation, Mesmer's work never achieved widespread recognition.

As more recent laboratory investigations into the physiological effects of laying on of hands have confirmed the magnetic nature of these subtle healing energies, researchers have demonstrated that Mesmer's understanding of the magnetic nature of the subtle energies of the human body was centuries ahead of his contemporaries. Direct measurement of these energies by conventional tools of electromagnetic detection are as difficult today as during Mesmer's time.

Mesmer also discovered that water could be charged with this subtle magnetic force and that the stored energy from bottles of healer-treated water could be transmitted to sick patients by way of metallic iron rods which the patients would hold in their hands. The storage device which was used to relay healing energy from the charged water to patients was known as the "bacquet". Although today many consider Mesmer to have been a great hypnotist, there are few who really understand the pioneering nature of his research into the subtle magnetic energies of healing.

Modern investigations into psychic healing

Over the last several decades scientific investigation into the medical effects of laying on of hands healing has shed new light on Mesmer's findings. In addition to confirming the actual exchange of energy between healer and patient which Mesmer and others suggested, researchers have demonstrated an interesting similarity between the biological effects of healers and high-intensity magnetic fields. The energetic fields of healers, although magnetic in character, also demonstrate other unique properties which have only recently begun to reveal themselves to scientific inquiry.

Recent experiments by Dr John Zimmerman with highly sensitive SQUID (Superconducting Quantum Interference Device) detectors, which can measure infinitesimally weak magnetic fields, have found increased magnetic field emission from the hands of psychic healers during healing. Yet these same, barely detectable healer-fields had powerful effects upon biological systems which could only be produced by treatment with the high-intensity magnetic fields.

This very elusive nature of the etheric fields is such that scientists today still have difficulty in measuring their presence, as did Benjamin Franklin in Mesmer's day. It is only through observation of their secondary effects on biological (enzymes), physical (crystallisation) and electronic systems (electrographic scanners) that science is beginning to amass evidential data on the validity of etheric energies. One indirect indication of the presence of the healing/etheric field is through its effect on increasing order within a system, i.e., its negative entropic drive.

A number of researchers have come to understand this negatively entropic property of healing energy. Dr Justa Smith's research suggested that healers have the ability to selectively affect different enzyme systems in a direction towards greater organisation and energy balance. By speeding up different enzymatic reactions, healers assist the body to heal itself. (This is also one of the great unrecognised principles of medicine. Doctors are only successful healers to the degree that they are able to use drugs, surgery, nutrition and various other means to assist the patients' innate healing mechanisms to repair their own sick bodies.) Healers provide a needed energetic boost to push the patient's total energetic system back into homeostasis. This healing energetic boost has special negatively-entropic, self-organisational properties that assist the cells in creating order from disorder along selectively defined routes of cellular expression.

An experiment was devised to test this negatively entropic property of the energy of healers. In Oregon, a multidisciplinary team met with Olga Worrall, a spiritual healer who had participated in Dr Smith's studies of healers, magnetic fields and enzymes. They wanted to test the hypothesis that healers enhance an organism's own ability to increase order. They speculated that a healer might also affect the self-organising properties of a special chemical reaction known as the Belousov-Zhabotinskii (B-Z) reaction. In the B-Z reaction, a chemical solution shifts between two states, which are indicated by unfolding, scroll-like spiral waves in a shallow Petri dish solution. If dyes are added to the solution, one observes an oscillation of colours from red to blue to red. This reaction is a special case of what is known as a "dissipative structure". (Ilya Prigogine won the 1977 Nobel prize for his Theory of Dissipative Structures, an innovative mathematical model which explains how systems like the B-Z reaction evolve to higher levels of order by using novel connections produced by entropy or disorder.)

Since the B-Z reaction is considered a self-organising chemical system, the research team wondered if the healer could affect its entropic status. Worrall was asked to try to affect a B-Z reaction. Following treatment by her healing hands, the solution produced waves at twice the speed of a control solution. In another experiment, the red–blue–red oscillation in two beakers of solution became synchronised after Worrall's treatments. The conclusion of the research team was that the healer's field was able to create greater levels of order in a non-organic system along the lines of negative entropic behaviour.

These results are consistent with the other studies like Dr Smith's which showed that healers (such as Olga Worrall) could cause UV-damaged enzymes to reintegrate to their normal structure and function. Enhanced growth in plants and faster wound-healing in mice are other examples of the healers' effect on increasing the organisation and order within cellular systems.

The diverse range of experimental data on the biological effects of healing is supportive of the hypothesis that a real energetic influence is exerted by healers on sick organisms. The biological systems examined in the previous experiments were all non-human in nature. Animal, plant and enzyme systems were utilised in hopes of removing any influence of suggestion or belief on the part of the test subject. Having validated the existence of a real therapeutic energy exchange between healers and non-human subjects, one is left to wonder about what actually occurs between healers and human patients.

If one accepts the fact that healers are able to induce measurable effects in living organisms, then one must ask important questions about the nature of healers in general. Are healers merely an elite group of humans in our society who possess a rare gift at birth? Or is healing an innate human potential which, like any other skill, might be enhanced by learning? If so, how does one go about teaching healing to others? Could healing be taught to individuals in the health-care professions to amplify their academically derived medical skills with natural energetic methods of therapeutic interaction? These questions have only recently begun to find meaningful answers. The growing impact of such issues reflects an undercurrent of subtle change in the evolving health-care field.

16
Relaxation through Expanded Awareness

◆

"In over twenty years of doing transformational work, I have found that the single most powerful technique for releasing stress and tension in the body and coming to true inner clarity is learning to make your body, senses and mind objects of observation," writes Dr Jim Dreaver in his book, *The Way of Harmony*. What follows in this chapter is based on Dr Dreaver's advice in the book:

In moments of quiet meditation or contemplation, practise looking at your body, its sensations and feelings, as well as the thoughts and images passing through your mind, as you would look at any other object – a tree, a cloud, a car.

It is a process of learning to become a dispassionate observer of your body, mind and senses. Doing this helps free you from identification with them. Instead of being caught up in your body and mind and looking out at the world from a place of relative conflict and contraction, pull your awareness back a little, to a place slightly behind and above your head. From there, begin to experience yourself as the space in which your body appears, in which breathing happens, in which sensations, feelings and thoughts arise. I call this way of observing, or experiencing your own body, mind and senses, "expanding awareness".

Health, then, is your natural state and your body's energies are always seeking their own organic harmony, or wholeness. When you are able to detach yourself from the areas of stress, tension and pain in your body and just be aware of them without the interference of your analytical mind, they have room to unwind and release. This is not to deny or ignore pain; it is to be present with it in a relaxed, open, non judging way. From this neutral place you can feel the length and breadth of your body within your awareness, your consciousness. You can observe the rising and falling of your breath. You can notice the space around your body. You can watch the movement of your arms, your legs, your head, your trunk within your visual and sensory field.

The more real this quality of awareness becomes for you, the more you find yourself in the expanded state of consciousness – the sense of ease, of flow, of well-being – that is your true nature. You feel very grounded in and connected to your body. All your senses are alert. You feel awake, clear, extraordinarily present. And behind it all is this tremendous feeling of spaciousness, of freedom.

Gradually, you begin to realise that you don't live in your body, as you had always believed, but your body lives in you. This is when you start to really achieve the core insight. It dawns on you that your true nature is pure consciousness, awareness, manifesting in this unique constellation of energy and matter that is your body/mind/self.

To see this is extremely liberating. It frees you from inner conflict and fear, including the fear of failure and even the fear of death, which means you can walk in the world with a much greater feeling of confidence.

Developing a relationship with your body

Your body is the vehicle for your spirit, the being you really are. Who you are is reflected in your body, in your muscles and joints, the way you breathe, sit, move.

To extend the vehicle analogy, imagine that you are taking a long trip in your car, but your car is a poorly serviced, unreliable clunker that is always breaking down. The trip wouldn't be much fun, would it? It is hard to enjoy the journey when you're constantly worried that your vehicle might not make it. That is why it is important to put energy into taking care of your body – so you can feel good moving around in it. When you do not feel good in your body – when you are tired, out-of-sorts, when your energy is contracted or stuck – it affects your attitude and makes you think all kinds of negative thoughts. On the other hand, when you have a sensitive and healthy relationship with your body, your attitude always improves.

You know what you need to do. You need to eat right, exercise and learn how to relax. The good news is that improving your physical wellbeing does not require a major change in your habits and actions. It's really more about a change in consciousness – the shifting of attention, or awareness, described above.

In learning to let go of the tension, worry and stress inside you, you will start to feel a whole lot better physically, and you will have more energy. It is psychological and emotional stress that is the real killer – much more so than eating the occasional fatty meal or not exercising for a week or two.

You will also be much less worried about or afraid of what is happening in your body. People fear unusual sensations or sudden changes in their bodily experience because they don't have a relationship with their bodies. Dr Dreaver remembers saying to a client once, "Bill, if you had a relationship with your wife like you have with your body, you'd be heading towards a divorce by now." "Don't get so divorced from your body that a doctor or therapist has to say that to you," Dr Dreaver comments! The best way to help your body do its job of keeping itself in balance is to develop a good relationship with it. That means to stop ignoring it, stop judging it and start treating it with kindness, affection and love just as you would a person you really cared about.

Becoming intimate with yourself

Trust in any relationship needs a certain level of intimacy. Trust itself leads to deeper intimacy. To become intimate with yourself, begin with your body. Start paying attention to the sensations and feelings in your body, to the movement of energy.

There is a saying in healing and bodywork circles: energy flows where attention goes. To generate new energy in some area of your life, just give that area more attention. If you want to liven up your marriage or relationship, give it more attention. If you want your work to be more successful, give that more attention. If you've planted a garden and want it to flourish, water it, weed it and care for it with love – then watch it grow. It is so simple!

To bring new energy into some part of your body, just expand your awareness of that area. To release shoulder tension, for example, bring your awareness into your shoulders and then consciously tighten them by hunching them all the way up around your ears. Breathe in as you do this. Then slowly release your shoulders, breathing out as you do so. Repeat this process several more times, loosely bounce your shoulders up and down and notice how much more energy you feel in them. This technique works because by intensifying the problem – the contraction – you are bringing it more into awareness, and that gives you more control over the muscles. It is a law of the body: heightened sensory awareness automatically brings about greater motor control. You can apply this principle to any tight muscle in your body. Just fully, consciously contract the selected muscle and then slowly release it. Notice the gradual flood of new sensation and feeling.

Relax and let go

Knowing how to relax, to really let go, is the key to being fully at ease in your body. One of the best ways of relaxing is to make breathing a conscious exercise. Slow it down to about half its normal rate and pause briefly between the in-breath and the out-breath. As your breathing slows down, it will become more effortless. Your whole metabolism will begin to calm down. Your pulse rate will drop and your blood pressure will lower. The body and mind are not separate. Uncomfortable body sensations cause the mind to worry and fret. Mental conflict, in turn, leads to emotional upset and creates stress in the body. When you learn how to relax your body, your mind will become quieter. There will be less chatter, less mental noise. You will start to tap into a deeper stillness and clarity. You will feel a natural balance within.

Practise relaxed breathing, then just be aware of the ever-changing sensations and feelings in your body. Try not to think about them. Just notice them. They will help you create more space inside your own consciousness. As a result, you'll feel more spacious and it will be much easier for you to deal with conflict and upsetting situations.

When people do not like what is happening in their experience, whether a condition in their body or a situation in their life, they usually go into immediate resistance and rejection, if not downright denial. If you are honest with yourself, you will acknowledge that you are probably familiar with this pattern.

But before you can change anything, you first have to accept it, to own it. When you are no longer fighting what is happening, you allow space for the seemingly stuck or uncomfortable energy to unwind and transform. You can practise this art of transformation through acceptance by beginning with your body. Learn to be a little detached from what you're experiencing in your body. This will give you some freedom from the experience. You will not be so caught up in it and it will be easier for you to deal with whatever is happening.

It is a welcoming of your experience. You are giving the situation or condition space to be. Then the knot of sensation that you have previously labelled "pain" or "tension" can loosen. A new awareness will emerge. To be aware of your body in this very sensitive, loving way is the most important step you can take in healing yourself physically. Learn to make pain your friend. Soften around it. Give it space to unwind. Even if the pain does not go away, the stress around it will lessen. It will become more manageable, more tolerable. Soften your belly, too. Notice how much tension gets held there. Let your belly relax and your whole being will breathe a sigh of relief.

In the light of clear, present awareness, where there is a calm acceptance of what is happening – rather than denial or resistance – consciousness expands. New insights enter your awareness, the problems at hand reveal their own solutions and things find their natural stability.

Ease and bliss

When you get really quiet and still, fully present in the moment, attuned to the subtlest movement of energy within and around you, the quickening life force causes a release of endorphins in your body. These are the hormones that dissolve pain and create pleasurable feelings, feelings of bliss, sometimes even ecstasy.

Bliss is what arises naturally when everything within you – body, mind, heart, soul – comes into perfect alignment or harmony. The energy of bliss is incredibly healing for the body. It softens, melts and eventually eliminates all the physical blocks and imbalances that cause pain, stiffness and inflammation. It brings a great sweetness to your life.

Tension and disease are the result of a dominant sympathetic nervous system, the fight-or-flight response that is the chief trait of chronic anxiety. As you learn to let go and simply relax, the parasympathetic nervous system takes over and floods the body with warm, blissful feelings.

A good healer knows how to stimulate the flow of healing energy in the patient's body. As your consciousness evolves and expands, you learn to become your own healer. You learn how to move and flex your body to release tension and holding, and then how to become perfectly still, so that you can open up to the deeper flow of life energy, the bliss that is your true bodily nature.

As your wisdom ripens, you will see that just as there is a wonderful upside to bliss, to the warm, melting sensations that you can create in your body, so there is also the danger of getting trapped by it. The bliss you get through moving your body, through making love or through sitting in deep meditation and communing with the spiritual energy behind creation can become another addiction, just like any drug. In time you will find the balance. Bliss will be a place you visit periodically, whenever you need healing and renewal from within, whenever you need to drink from the well, the source of life, again. This may be once or several times a day, for a few minutes or for longer. Once you have made the connection, then it will be time to plunge back into everyday life and get on with the ever-important work of creating, relating, loving and serving.

In any case, whenever you pause in your activities and consciously attune to the underlying rhythm and flow of the universe, bliss will be there. You will feel it as the essence of your being, the very substance of who and what you are.

You will notice that as you become more conscious and feel more at ease in your body, you'll bring through more life force. Your movements will be more graceful and you will radiate vitality. When you're not consciously connected to your body, you will tend to move awkwardly, be clumsy, have accidents. If these things are happening to you, take heed. Be present. Be in your body.

You need some form of daily movement and stretching to help keep your body supple, to keep the energy moving through you. It does not take a lot, either. It is the quality of movement that counts, not the quantity. There are many useful practices that foster conscious breathing, movement and body-centring. They teach you how to move your own energy and stay grounded in your body.

Yoga, somatic (mind/body) exercises, dance and martial arts are examples of such practices. Chiropractic, massage, bodywork and movement education are also good tools for helping you get more connected with your body. The more relaxed and present you are in your body, the less likely you are to be overtaken by fear, anger, depression and other negative emotional states.

Remember, too, that it's not how your body looks that matters. People get too hung up on images and appearances. Our society is filled with people who have shapely, buffed bodies, who wear the right clothes, live in the right houses, drive the right cars, have the right jobs and yet are not happy. Their minds are filled with conflict and discontent, their hearts are empty, their souls are anguished, there is little or no love in their lives.

What really matters is how you feel in your body. By all means look your best (looking good is very much a part of the balance), but give even more attention to getting your internal energy flowing in a nourishing way.

Start accepting the fact that there is really only one energy – the creative energy of life itself, the core vibration of the universe, the incredible and mysterious power we call "spirit", "God" or "life force". When you know how to relax and truly open up to it, you feel that vibration in your body as ease, bliss, wellbeing. You experience it in your mind as clarity, wisdom, meaning. You feel it in your heart as unity, love, joy.

Open up to who and what you truly are. Become a fine-tuned instrument for divine energy, for spiritual power. Let the energy of love shine through your eyes and through the pores of your skin. Then, no matter what others think of you, you will feel good inside – and people will ultimately be attracted to that far more than they will to your outer appearances, Dr Dreaver concludes.

17
The Healing Power of Faith

Healing can include dramatic, sudden physical cures, but is not confined to the "miraculous" or the spectacular, according to Harold Koenig, MD.

Perhaps for most people, the healing power of faith involves a healing of the mind and emotions, the intangible spirit, and of relationships with others. Faith can put physical illness beneath us, where it belongs, return dominion to us and give us power to live victorious and fulfilling lives. People who regularly attend church service, pray individually and read the Bible, are 40 per cent less likely to have diastolic hypertension than those who seldom participate in these religious activities.

People who attend religious services regularly may have stronger immune systems than their less religious counterparts. Those who never or rarely attend church or synagogue tend to have the highest levels of Interleukin-6, perhaps indicating a weakened or overactive immune system. People who attend church regularly are hospitalised less often and leave the hospital sooner than people who never or rarely participate in religious services. The deeper a person's religious faith, the less likely they are to be crippled by depression during and after hospitalisation for physical illness.

Religious people have healthier lifestyles. According to one study, people who attend church at least weekly have about one third the rate of alcohol abuse and are about a third as likely to smoke as those who seldom participate in congregational worship.

Religious youth show significantly lower levels of drug and alcohol abuse, premature sexual involvement and criminal delinquency than their non-religious peers. They are also less likely to express suicidal thoughts or make actual attempts on their lives.

Elderly people with a deep, personal religious faith have a stronger sense of wellbeing and life satisfaction than their less religious peers. Religious people live longer and physically healthier lives than their non-religious counterparts.

18

Increase Your Healing Ability

◆

Everyone is a healer, according to Marie T. Russell. Just as everyone is alive and breathing, everyone has the power and the ability to connect with the life energy that brings in healing. You do not need training, though you can certainly learn techniques and earn confidence by taking classes; you don't need certification, though, if you're going to become a "healer" officially and provide your services for hire, then certification is recommended. But if you're wanting to increase your healing ability so that you can use it for your own healing, then it is right there waiting for you to tap into it.

Many of us go through life seeking healing from other people when really the only person who can heal us is ourselves. We run to doctors or healers to have them "heal" us. Yet the body is the one which heals itself with the aid of whatever remedies or assistance it receives. Whether one is taking pills, vitamins or herbs, the body is the one that utilises these as it sees fit. You could be eating the best foods, yet your body has to know and be capable of utilising them in order for you to be "healed".

The body is the one which knows what to do with the calcium, the vitamins, the enzymes, the healing energy... If it did not have its own innate intelligence, it would not know how to utilise these healing substances that we ingest and accept into our being. The medicines or the medical staff are not the healers... the body itself is the healer. Thus, the responsibility for healing returns to its only true home, yourself. Possibly you ! in healing yourself and you feel you don' start. A good place to start is with cor that you indeed can heal yourself. This r ming the thoughts you carry of lack... l; self-worth and self-confidence. You might beg-programming with statements such as these:

- My body is healing itself and the cells of my body are constantly "giving birth" to new healthy cells.
- Every day, I get healthier and happier (and whatever other qualifications you may want to increase in your life).
- My body is constantly healing itself every day and every moment. Every little cell in my body is happy; every little cell in my body is well.
- I am connected with the life force and always have enough energy and vitality to be completely healthy and happy.

Practise talking to yourself – If you are afraid of being thought weird, speak silently to yourself. Talk to the cells of your body. Tell them you love them. Tell them you now give them permission to be healthy. Visualise them being healthy and vibrant with life force. See your body being filled with radiant healing energy. Feel it spreading from the top of your head down to the bottom of your feet. Tell yourself that you now give yourself complete permission to be 100 per cent healthy and 100 per cent happy.

How to do hands-on self-healing – You can do "hands-on" healing on yourself. All you need is the willingness to accept that this is indeed possible and to give permission to have Divine energy flow through you.

Start by asking for Divine protection and see yourself surrounded by white light. A good way to do this is to fill your heart with white light and then have the light expanding until you are filled with it, and surrounded with light in a somewhat egg-shaped glow. Hold your left hand up, palm outward, and ask for healing energy to flow through you. Imagine the healing energy coming into your body through the palm of your left hand. You can visualise it as white light, or green energy, or whatever seems appropriate to you at the given moment. Trust your intuition or gut feeling on this one, as different healing situations will call for different energies, or colours of light, or warmth, etc.

As you keep holding your left hand up and allowing the Divine energy to enter, place your right hand, palm down, on the area of your body which needs healing. You may feel some warmth entering your left hand, and the palm of your right hand may get hot. You might also feel a tingling or vibrating effect. This is the energy of healing moving through you. (If you do not feel anything, do not worry. The energy is still there – you simply are not sensitive to it yet.)

Relax and be grateful for the ability to be a channel for this energy. You may use this for digestion problems, muscle soreness, tense shoulders, headaches, stress, etc. You may also use this God-given talent to share with friends. Teach them to connect with this force. Everyone is a healer. The body was built as a self-healing mechanism. When given the chance the body heals itself. Animals know this which is why they go off by themselves to rest when hurt or ill. The human animal (that is us) can also do the same. We can respect the needs of our body for quiet, rest, fasting and healing energy. Listen to the quiet inner voice which guides you as to what you need to do. When feeling ill you may choose to take some time to be alone and quietly apply some healing energy to your body. After all, this body is the only one you have got. When it is properly connected to life energy it can heal itself, so plug in to the source and heal thyself...

19
Healing Intuition

◆

"I am often asked to explain what intuition is," writes psychologist Carol Ritberger, Ph.D. "People are curious about what it feels like and they want to know how it expresses itself. They also want to know when they are using it. And, most important, they want to know how they can develop the trust in it that is necessary to follow its direction. I find that describing intuition is easier than trying to put it into definitive terms, because it expresses itself differently in each person. We are so conditioned to using our five physical senses (sight, hearing, touch, taste and smell) that we expect intuition to be something equally tangible. We expect it to be black and white and it is not. Intuition is the sensory process that reveals its information through the pictures it paints in our minds and the quiet inner voice that we hear throughout our body. The five physical senses are easy to understand and relate to. Intuition – the 'sixth sense' – requires us to trust, not to know."

Are you intuitive by nature?

Every single one of us is an intuitive being. A person does not have to be psychic to be intuitive or to use their intuition for the purpose of diagnostic analysis of the body. Intuition is one of our natural instincts and is a critical part of our mental processing. In fact, it is so integral that most of the time we take it for granted or are not even aware that we are utilising it. Intuitive mental processing is usually associated with right-brain functioning. However, it is really whole-brain thinking. We utilise our intuition as a means of providing a different way to look at situations, as a means of getting a well-rounded perspective on what is happening, says Dr Ritberger.

Intuition is like a weather gauge. It tells us what the current conditions are and alerts us when change is in the air. It is the vehicle through which our spirit expresses itself to our external world. It sees the situations and challenges that life throws our way from a holistic point of view. It is the conceptual part of our thinking and is what allows the mind to create ideas. Its spark kindles the flame and fuels the fires that drive us to manifest our dreams. Its energy provides the inspiration needed to encourage us to follow our visions. The use of intuition encourages us to look at possibilities and explore the unknown.

Intuition can often provide the answers to problems when the conscious mind cannot. It does not express itself through the five senses or the left part of our brain, but rather through the pictures, dreams, memories, feelings and impressions that are stored in the right brain. Intuitive information reveals itself to the conscious mind in the form of emotions, which are then chemically communicated to the physical body through reactions such as hunches, gut feelings, sudden bursts of insight, or flashes of awareness out of the blue. For example, have you ever known someone was going to call even before they do? Or got an idea and just knew that it was a sure-fire winner? Or struggled with a problem only to find the solution in a dream? That was intuition in action, writes Dr Ritberger.

How to develop intuitive skills

Another question that people ask me is what can they do to develop or hone their intuitive skills, says Dr Ritberger. The first and most obvious answer is to create an awareness around it. Pay attention to how it expresses itself. Then practise integrating it into your daily life so that you will become comfortable with it. The more you use it, the more you will trust it, as well as the information it provides. Another important element in the development of your intuitive skills is not to work hard at being intuitive. Intuition is not something that can be accessed when your mind is active or outwardly focused. It requires a relaxed mind and a relaxed body. Your focus must be internal and introspective. The information it can provide must be allowed to flow freely. It requires time and lack of expectations so it can look at the situation or problem from all perspectives.

The integration of intuition into your daily life heightens your sensory awareness. It empowers you and it expands your consciousness. It opens up a whole new way of looking at life and prepares you to cope with change. It reduces the amount of anxiety and fear in your life. They are two of our most powerful emotions and capable of creating stress in the physical body and imbalance in the energy body. They are precursors to the creation of illness, writes Dr Ritberger.

Become your own diagnostician

The energy system is very effective in communicating its state of health. With a little practice, you can perform your own diagnostic check-up. How? The fastest way is by learning to let your hands read your energy field. The hands, and particularly the fingertips, are very sensitive instruments that can scan the physical body to feel where imbalances are occurring. If the energy system is strong and vital, then you will feel an overall warmth over the areas being examined. However, if there is congestion or energy depletion, then you will feel cold spots or there will be areas where you can barely feel any heat at all. If there is chemical over-stimulation of an endocrine gland or an energetic protrusion, then the affected area will feel very warm or hot, according to Dr Ritberger.

"Let me share an example to help you understand how the energy system and the physical body affect each other. Let's say you are in a conversation where you are trying to express your thoughts on a particular topic. The problem is that the person you are talking to cannot seem to understand what you are trying to say or cannot appreciate the importance of the point you're trying to make. The more you try to get your point across, the more frustrated you become. As your frustration increases, so does your stress level. This emotional reaction causes the energy system to sound the alarm and warn the body that the reaction is in fact having a negative impact on the physical body," Dr Ritberger comments.

Now, let us say your frustration turns to anger. The more angry you become, the greater the severity of chemical imbalance in your body. The physical result is that your throat tightens up. The minute this happens, you begin to have difficulty swallowing – perhaps you cough or choke or your voice breaks. These physical reactions are the energy system's way of trying to tell the body to shut down what is creating the imbalance. If you were to scan the throat area at the time this was happening, you would feel a large hot spot (protrusion) of energy in this area. Then, as the emotional reaction subsided, the energy in this area would return to normal and you would just feel a warmth around the throat.

"I believe that each of us can become an intuitive diagnostician to some extent," says Dr Ritberger. All that is required is that we evolve our intuition to the point where it allows us to read the energy system for the purpose of gathering information and perceiving any malfunctions in the body. With some practice and patience, any person can hone their intuitive skills in such a way that they can accurately read where energy imbalances are occurring in the body. However, there is one important element that you must adhere to if you are to become an accurate diagnostician, and that is the ability to emotionally detach from the person you are reading – not an easy thing to do, especially if the person you are trying to read is yourself. Yet without the ability to emotionally detach, you contaminate the quality of the information your intuition provides. You will distort the information so it feels safe, or negate what it is telling you as not being valid.

The best way to start the process of becoming your own diagnostician is to learn how to read your own energy and body. Start by paying attention to how your intuition communicates with you. Does it reveal itself through your instinctive feelings? Perhaps it is a gut feeling or a sudden flash insight, or maybe even those goose bumps you get when you "just know that you know". Pay attention to the impressions that your intuition sends you. Listen to how it tells you that something is out of sync. When you get those feelings, ask your intuition where in the body you are out of sync and what is causing it. If you pay attention, it will even tell you what is needed in order to restore balance. When you are using your intuition to read your body, it is always important to trust your first impressions. They will tell you precisely what is happening within the body. Do not dismiss any impression even if it is disturbing. The impressions you receive first provide a clear picture of what is really occurring, as they have not yet been distorted by your emotions. If you get the message that something is wrong, then act on that information. Your first impressions will always serve you well, and nine times out of ten they will be right, according to Dr Ritberger.

You do not have to literally see the human energy system in order to be an energetic diagnostician. You can develop a skill called symbolic sight. In fact, many gifted healers and intuitive diagnosticians work from symbolic sight. Symbolic sight is where you look for the symbolism of what is happening in your life and connect that symbolism to what is happening within your physical body. For example, when you feel that life is beating you up, then your body responds by feeling beaten up and tired. When craving for sweets, then maybe one is craving for sweets in other parts of one's life such as self-esteem, financial abundance, love and relationships. Breathing problems symbolise the feeling of being stifled. Being financially strapped shows up in the lower back. Inability to face life shows up through mental illness. Never being good enough manifests as auto-immune diseases and anaemia.

Diagnostic keys

Learn to listen to your emotions. Spend time with them. Do not rush to hide them or make them go away. Emotions provide direction. They are indicators that send very clear messages of how you are feeling both energetically and physically. If you are feeling positive and optimistic, then your energy level increases and your whole body responds by feeling good. If you are feeling depressed, then your energy level decreases; your body becomes tired and lethargic. Confusion causes a chemical imbalance in the brain and your thinking becomes cloudy. The feeling of being out of control causes an energy loss throughout your entire body. Resentment drains energy from your stomach area. The feeling of being taken advantage of causes a loss of energy in your heart. Anger toward others drains the lower extremities of energy. Your emotions can even tell you if you're holding on to old emotional hurts and if you are using those hurts to manipulate others so as to get what you want or to make them feel sorry for you. Begin to pay attention to how you interact with the people in your life: family, friends and co-workers. Do you surround yourself with people who energise you or drain you? How do you react emotionally to these types of people? Do the people in your life support you, or do they want you to be dependent on them? Do they enable you to stay emotionally wounded, or do they encourage growth and change? Always listen to your intuition when it comes to dealing with others. It will provide a clear picture of what is really happening. Learn to read your behavioural patterns when around others. If your behaviour is submissive, then you will attract people who will want to control you. If the message you send out is that you are emotionally vulnerable, then people will sense that and take advantage of you. Is your behaviour telling people that you are a victim? If so, that might help explain why you keep attracting individuals who are domineering and aggressive.

Body scanning

Take a daily pulse check of your energy level by doing a body scan. The body-scanning process allows your intuition to participate in your energetic evaluation. It also hones your skill to become sensitive to energetic imbalances. Through the scanning process, you will receive indications as to where you are both energetically and physically. Ritberger has found that his morning meditation is the best time for him. Start at your head or crown and work your way down all the way to your toes. Spend time in each section of the body. Run your hands over each part to locate any energy protrusion or depletion. The body is very effective in communicating where there are any imbalances. It will usually convey these imbalances physically through our aches and pains and areas where we feel discomfort. If a blockage is occurring, then there will usually be some kind of inflammation or heat build-up in that particular part of your body.

The technique of body scanning also fully utilises your intuitive awareness by drawing attention to the impressions it sends. When you get an impression that alerts you that there is something out of balance, spend time with that impression. Determine where in the body you are sensing it. For example, if you are scanning the body intuitively and get an impression that your stomach is on fire, spend time exploring why it is occurring in this area. Ask yourself some questions. Could the imbalance be caused by something you ate? Have you been under a lot of stress lately, and is this where you are carrying your stress issues? Have you been suffering from frequent indigestion for a prolonged period of time? Is the severity of the discomfort enough to cause your mind to become alarmed? If so, then it is probably time to have it checked out by a physician or a holistic practitioner, depending on your belief system. Remember, the body will tell you what it needs; you just have to take the time to listen.

You can also keep an energy journal. This will help track your energy cycles. Each of us has them. Some of us are morning people, while others are night owls. Some people get their day started energetically at three o'clock in the afternoon, while others are ready for a nap. Know when you feel energised and when you are energetically low. Begin paying attention to what or who drains your energy, and if at all possible, stay away from those things or people when you are in a low cycle. Avoid tasks that require large amounts of energy to be expended in your down times. Stay away from having to deal with emotional issues when you are feeling low. It is too draining and the results will be less than desired. Also, never deal with emotional issues before you go to sleep, or you will wake up the next day energetically drained and physically tired. Try to deal with emotional issues when you are in your high-energy cycle. When you first start the process of being your own diagnostician, it may take a bit of getting used to. If you give yourself time, it will become second nature to you. You will find the rewards to be many. There is one thing, though, that I must warn you about: once you allow your intuition to become an active part of your life, you will change. But change is what life is about anyway, isn't it?

Judith Orloff is a medical doctor who is also intuitive. Her first book, *Second Sight*, was a highly personal account of her efforts to merge two aspects of herself, the side which has been intuitive since childhood and the side which represents a family tradition of doctors. *Second Sight* was a coming out of sorts, a proclamation of her truth. The response to her first book left her with shopping bags full of unanswered letters from people seeking her help. She has begun to train other professionals to assist in tending to the overwhelming response. Even the medical profession is interested in her work. She has addressed the American Psychiatric Association Convention, the largest gathering of mainstream psychiatrists in the USA. She is the first "intuitive" to be invited to address this prestigious conference.

Her subsequent book, *Dr Judith Orloff's Guide to Intuitive Healing*, was a further effort to reach those seeking to learn about intuitive healing physically, emotionally and sexually.

From the moment we are born, Dr Orloff reasons, we are trained to think and analyse. Children are never taught the value of silence and of listening to their bodies. We don't have the same beliefs as the Aboriginals and the native American cultures where, from the day the baby is born, the whole concept of dreaming, intuition and visioning is part of the community. In Western culture, there is a poverty of vision and that is why it is so hard for people to remember they can "see". In writing the *Guide to Intuitive Healing*, she says her goal was to help people rethink this evolutionary ability that they have repressed. Intuition, she believes, can bring us into joy, health and exuberance. "I don't believe people can reach their full potential, in the deepest sense, without connecting to this aspect of themselves," she discloses. "I work in Los Angeles and I have a lot of patients who come to me from the film industry. They come in lost. They can't make decisions or connect with other people. Part of the work we do is connecting them with their inner voice so they know they have something valuable inside. When they find this jewel, which is their intuitive voice, they find they have something very real that will tell them the truth about things. It's the opposite of getting fixed on the outside through such things as jobs, sex, food, psychics or even spiritual teachers who will tell them what to do. When they begin to trust their inner voice it doesn't matter what they are facing. Their intuition acts as an antidote to fear. It's like when my father was dying and I was certain that I wouldn't be able to help him face his death alone, but the voice inside of me said, 'I can do this, I can help my father die,' and I knew I was up to the job."

Dr Orloff has said that she had so much fear about coming out as an intuitive doctor, it took her seven years to write *Second Sight*. She worried about what her peers would think. She had a writer's block. She was afraid she might be run out of the medical profession. But, she had such a belief in this work that her passion for it won out. "Now that I have come out and I see the good that can be done, I'm unstoppable..."

The immediate response to her books was that she suddenly had four thousand people on her patient waiting list. "I'll never forget it. I started getting these letters and calls saying 'your life is my life.' Physicians, nurses, teachers and housewives, all saying, 'This is me,' or 'I've had this happen to me and I've been afraid to talk about it because I was afraid people would think I'm crazy.'"

Dr Orloff has spoken before gatherings of about 18,000 psychiatrists on how intuition can enhance patient care. She does not try to convince them. She simply tells them how intuition has worked with her patients and gives examples.

When promoting her *Dr Judith Orloff's Guide to Intuitive Healing: Five Steps to Physical, Emotional and Sexual Wellness*, a woman came up to her holding an envelope and said, "If you're so intuitive, tell me what the number is inside this envelope." Dr Orloff responds: "When it happens I have to explain that I use my intuition for love and service. My intuition doesn't work with lottery numbers."

Dr Orloff maintains that the intuitive tools she teaches about in her new book work for her because they are fuelled by love. She says we must believe in the power of love above all else in the universe, and everything she does is motivated by that.

"If love isn't the motivating force the power is very muted. Love gives intuitive energy. No matter what your question is, if you don't have the answer, you can always depend on love. If you don't know what to do, the answer always comes from the heart. The answer is always love. That's the bottom line."

Dr Orloff hopes that this book will teach people to

open their hearts, begin to love themselves and begin to trust that they have a very precious intuitive voice inside that will guide them in everything they do. They are not alone. They can contact this precious voice for help with whatever they are going through in life and it will tell them the truth about how they can proceed. It will also give them a link to a loving, compassionate spiritual presence that will surround them. They will see the basic connection between all living things and know that our great strength lives in the circle of love that binds us together.

"If you are dealing with a disease or chronic illness, you'll have many decisions to make regarding your options for care," writes Dr Orloff. "Should you undergo open heart surgery? Medication or meditation? Whatever condition or disease you are dealing with, your intuition can be a valuable tool in deciding what treatment is right for you. But how can you quiet the hubbub of well-meaning voices (physicians, family, friends, even your manicurist) that threaten to drown out the voice of your intuition? As illustrated in my book, *Dr Judith Orloff's Guide to Intuitive Healing*, the following five tactics can help you access that unbiased inner authority, your intuition."

Notice your beliefs

Does this sound familiar? "What did I do wrong? Why me? It's hopeless. It's unfair. I'm a victim." If so, you've got to change your mindset, or your internalised belief system, and put it to work so it is healing, not harmful. When you hear these negative voices, say "Thanks for sharing," and move on.
In all types of illness, from cancer to a cold, never fail to remember the mind's capacity to heal even what has been deemed "unhealable". By lovingly learning to refocus

your intuition, you can strive to cure or at least improve any health situation.

The following exercise can help you articulate your beliefs about healing and illness and, if necessary, can help you change them. Ask yourself:

- Do your beliefs give you strength during illness? If not, are you ready to find ones that do?
- In a health crisis, what role does your intuition play? How far would you trust it?
- How do you treat yourself when you're sick or in pain? If you're self-critical, how can you turn this into self-compassion?
- Do you believe love can heal? How about humour? Are you willing to put them to the test?

Be in your body

Our tendency, once we feel pain or get sick, is to check out of our bodies ("That's it, I'm out of here!") But to do so is to ignore two intuitive truths. Intuitive truth number one is that the more love and consciousness you bring to your body, the better chance you'll have of mending it. Intuitive truth number two says that if you resist discomfort, it will persist. But if you soften around it, it will lessen.

When you are in tune with your body, there's no guarantee that your pain will miraculously dissipate, though it just might. What will happen, however, is that you will enter into a relationship with a force that can provide clues on how to heal. This is a very different philosophy from just swallowing a pill, sitting back and waiting for the pain to go away.

The following meditation for dealing with pain and illness can help you access the healing powers that come from paying attention to your body:

1. Relax into the discomfort. Simply let the pain be.

2. Intuitively tune in to the discomfort. Does it have colour? Texture? Temperature? Ask the discomfort: What can I learn from you? How can I ease my pain?

3. Feel your discomfort completely. As you inhale, breathe in all your pain. Visualise it as a cloud of dark smoke. Now picture the dark smoke being purified by your reserves of love and compassion. Exhale, letting the dark smoke flow out of your body in the form of clear white light.

Sense your body's subtle energy

Never underestimate your energy's ability to ease suffering, accelerate healing or even cure disease. Our bodies are composed of energy centres known as chakras. For the purposes of the following meditation, we'll focus on the heart chakra, the main generator that fuels our healing system. The heart chakra is located in the middle of your chest, over the diaphragm. To activate it, try the meditation for opening the heart:

1. Be very quiet. Relax your body and focus on your breathing. Gently place your hand over your heart chakra and hold it there. Now get ready to visualise.

2. Concentrate on a person, place or animal that you really love. Focus on feeling love and notice how its energy equivalent localises in your mid-chest.

3. Pay attention to sensations such as warmth, cold or tingling in your heart chakra. As you practise, a vortex of positive energy in your heart chakra will build. This is the hub of your healing. During times of pain or illness, tap into it.

Also, you may find it useful to practise sharing energy with a friend. To do so, place your hands over a friend's chest. Focus on feeling your heart chakra opening. Spend a few minutes allowing love to go freely from your heart, down your arms, out of your palms and into your friend. Then reverse roles. You'll discover that love nourishes you as much as it does the person you are healing.

Ask for inner guidance

When you have a diagnosis and are ready to make treatment decisions, gather as much information as you can about your illness, but do not stop there. Take all the time you need to listen intuitively. No matter how impressive the scientific evidence, your choice must sit well with you. Asking yourself the following questions can help you access your intuition as you make these important decisions:

- What does my gut say? Is it tied in knots or relaxed? Does an option feel "right" or "off"?

- Do I sleep better or worse at night thinking about a particular approach? Does going ahead with it make me feel more at peace?

- When I quietly tune in, what images or impressions come to me? Are they telling me to go ahead? Wait? Seek out another alternative? Pose specific questions to your intuition. Evaluate the response.

How do you know if your intuitions are accurate? Can you separate them from your hopes and fears? To make sure the process is pure, pay attention to those messages that are either completely neutral, with no emotional charge, or those conveyed with compassion. I've come to depend on these factors to gauge reliability.

Listen to your dreams

In our world, science's vigilant effort to quantify illness could profit by collaborating with dreams. Relegating hard science to one camp and visionary dreams to another is a no-win proposition for everyone. The two can work together. Dreaming is hinged on the surrender of our thinking minds. More healing is possible without our ordinary walls intact when creativity is at its peak. Healing equals creativity. In terms of your body, dreams offer brilliant solutions to health issues that may have never dawned on you before. There are indications of whether a healing dream is intuitively accurate. The following are tried-and-true touchstones:

- exceptionally vibrant imagery, colours, or sounds
- an oddly impersonal tone, neutrally imparting information
- a sense of indisputable "knowing" in your body
- a crispness and clarity to segments.

The following four tips on intuitive dream interpretations can help you get the most out of your dreams:

1. On awakening, record your dream immediately in a journal.
2. Notice those images and dream symbols to which you're especially drawn or those that move you.
3. As soon as possible, go into meditation. Hold the symbol in your mind. Specifically ask to be shown its significance.
4. Pay particular attention to any images, scenarios, memories or physical sensations that arise. These intuitions come from the deepest part of you. They will explain your symbol.

20
Intuitive Diagnosis

---◆---

Throughout history, writes Carol Ritberger, Ph.D., there is evidence that medical intuition has been used for diagnosis. The first recorded writings of such skills were by the Pythagoreans in 500 BC They held that there was a luminous body of light around a person that could produce a variety of effects in the human body, including the causing and the curing of illnesses. These ancient Greeks were known for their uncanny knack for intuiting the nature of things. It was also in 500 BC that Hippocrates first proposed a comprehensive mind and body theory linking health, illness and personality. In the sixteenth century, it was Paracelsus, an alchemist and physician, who used intuition and his ability to read energy as part of his diagnostic process. He called the energy he saw Illistar, and the information contained within this energy revealed where in the body illness was occurring. In the 1800s, Franz Anton Mesmer introduced the technique that came to be known as mesmerism. Mesmer discovered that patients who entered a trance state were able to use their intuition to access a different level and quality of information. It is his work that eventually became the foundation for psychiatry and psychology. It was not, however, until the nineteenth century that the first formal study of intuitive diagnosis occurred using mesmerism as the foundation.

The study was conducted by Dr John Elliotson, a British physician who used the technique of mesmerising to entrance and anaesthetise his subjects. While in this state, he found that they could use their intuition to access information for the purpose of identifying illnesses. Elliotson would take his mesmerised subjects to hospitals and ask them to use their intuition to identify illnesses that were baffling physicians. The accuracy with which they could diagnose illness was both uncanny and astonishing. Needless to say, when Elliotson reported his findings to his conservative colleagues in the medical profession, they were not openly embraced. His innovative ideas and his approach did not fit within the parameters of traditional medicine.

In 1911, Dr William Kilner, a medical doctor, reported his findings on the use of intuition as a means of exploring the human energy system. Kilner found that the "aura" differed considerably from patient to patient depending on sex, mental ability and health. His studies showed there was a direct connection between illness and what he would see in the energy system. He found that certain diseases showed up as patches or irregularities of energy within the energy field. He used this information to diagnose a variety of ailments, such as liver dysfunction, tumours, epilepsy and psychological disturbances.

The most widely known medical intuitive diagnostician, Edgar Cayce (1877–1945), who was known as "The Sleeping Prophet", used his intuitive insight for the purpose of medical diagnoses. While Cayce was able to read many aspects of a person intuitively, his focus was centred on the health of the energy body and the physical body. Cayce gave extensive readings on the effects of attitudes and emotions on one's health. He emphasised that negatively charged emotions released toxins from the glandular system of the body. He stated that these toxins would create imbalances that would deplete one's energy. They would block the elimination process and generally make a person more susceptible to the creation of disease. Cayce also professed that anger created stomach problems and headaches, that depression weakened the immune system, and that fear was the root cause of heart problems. In his writings, he discussed the interrelationship between stress and disease. He discussed the human energy system and its holographic imaging of the physical body.

Cayce considered each "entity" (what he called a person) to have three aspects of energy – physical, mental and spiritual. He believed the mind and body to be vehicles through which the spirit could express itself externally. Cayce suggested that all illnesses are the result of overloads and blockages in these three aspects of energy. In one of his readings, Cayce said, "Healing of the physical without change in the mental and spiritual aspects brings little real help to the individuals in the end." It is Edgar Cayce's work and the information gathered through his readings that has laid the groundwork for contemporary intuitive diagnosticians to follow. His work resulted in some of the most comprehensive studies ever done on the connection between health and spirituality.

Since Edgar Cayce's time, there have been many other gifted healers and intuitive diagnosticians who have come forward to share their unique skills. Each has brought forth their own individual means of expressing how they use their intuition for diagnostic purposes. Some of these people include Dr Edward Bach, Olga Worrall, Louise L. Hay, Dr Robert Leitchman, Dr John Pierrakos, Barbara Ann Brennan, Mona Lisa Schulz and Dr Caroline Myss. I am sure that there are many others who are very skilled in intuitive diagnoses who are quietly doing their work to help people understand the relationship between the human energy system and illness. If you are one of them, I encourage you to come forward. The need is greater than the supply.

Reading the physical body

As a diagnostic tool, the human energy system acts as an imaging and monitoring system that reflects all changes occurring within the energy body and the physical body. When there is illness (imbalance) in the energy body, it communicates this information by creating blockages, protrusions, congestion or depletion within the energy field. Any time these energetic factors occur, there is potential for the physical body to become susceptible to infection or disease.

The human energy system is designed to act as an early detection system alerting the brain and the cells of the body that something is out of sync. When the brain receives a message from the human energy system that imbalance is occurring, it sends out electrical impulses to the specific site within the body where there is imbalance. The depth of information that the human energy system can provide to the brain is very substantial. It can provide feedback to pinpoint the origin of the imbalance. It can also provide feedback on the condition created by the imbalance and its severity. Since the energy body and the physical body mirror each other, the energy system will instantly reflect what is changing and how that change is affecting the physical body.

When the energy body becomes ill, there are two distinct ways in which that illness will surface in the physical body. The first is that there will be an overall feeling of energy loss. The energy field will actually reduce its size in order to protect the healthy energy it has left. The physical body reacts by becoming tired. Second, the energy system tells the brain to send messages via the endocrine system, alerting the physical body that something is out of balance. The endocrine system communicates the imbalance by secreting a variety of chemicals that affect both the nervous system and the immune system. The physical body reacts by creating either a mild or extreme stress reaction. The physical results are an adrenaline rush, increased heartbeat and a change in breathing patterns. If the imbalance is mild, then the physical body responds in subtle ways, which may include mild headaches, indigestion or muscle tension. However, if the imbalance is extreme or continues for a prolonged period of time (meaning that it becomes chronic), then the body may progress to the point of complete physical breakdown.

It should be noted that not every change in the energy system ends up manifesting itself into a physical dysfunction. The fact is that we are always changing the body's physiology for better or worse every second of our lives. Since the energy system is a dynamic force, there are many situations we experience daily that cause it to change and fluctuate. For the most part, many of those changes go unnoticed. The primary factor that determines if any change manifests itself into a physical dysfunction is our emotional reaction to those changes. If our emotional reaction is negative or we are resistant to the change, then the energy system will sound the alert and the physical body will respond accordingly.

The willingness to change

Over the course of reading the human energy system and working with people to help them better understand the relationship between their energy system, their emotions and their illnesses, an interesting truth has presented itself, which is: while many people say they want to be healed, most are not willing to change the emotional and psychological patterns that lead to the creation of their illness.

21

How to Befriend Your Pain

◆

"Sometimes your pain doesn't make your life unbearable; your life makes your pain unbearable," wrote Dr David Bresler, Ph.D. The word pain is derived from the Latin word *poena*, which means punishment. Whether pain should be thought of as a punishment is debatable, but we know that it certainly hurts to have it, and it usually feels like a punishment, whether the person has done something to deserve it or not. In ancient times, people thought that pain was caused by demons who had possessed them. And if you didn't pay your exorcist to get rid of the demons, you got repossessed!

Pain is nature's way of making you take notice. It is a warning – sometimes a loud warning – that something is wrong. It is a symptom and a signal, and it demands your attention!

"Headaches, backaches, arthritis and menstrual cramps are the most frequent pain syndromes. Most people today treat their pain with one or more of the various anti-inflammatory medicines, a.k.a. painkillers," writes Dana Ullman, M.Ph. "However, because pain itself is only a symptom, painkillers may reduce the discomfort but do nothing to heal the source of pain. In fact, suppressing the symptoms of pain can drive the pain and the disease deeper into the person. The body eventually adapts to the painkillers and soon needs stronger and stronger doses in order to achieve a similar degree of relief. The body also becomes addicted to these drugs, ultimately causing new types of discomfort and dysfunction for which a person all too often takes additional drugs. A pain cycle has been created and it is sometimes difficult to break."

Denying pain

Denying pain is equally ineffective. Some people ignore their pain. They assume that nothing is wrong, that there is nothing that they should change about themselves and that the pain they are having is only a temporary glitch that will soon disappear.

Famed psychiatrist Carl Jung once said, "If you don't come to terms with your shadow, it will appear in your life as your fate." Until a person sheds light on the shadow of pain, its fateful return will be a continual reminder of something amiss. Denial runs deep and wide, and you cannot wash away your pain by denial. Unless and until awareness replaces denial, the pain will demand attention one way or another.

What is it saying?

The challenge of pain is to try to comprehend what it is saying. What is not in balance in your life? Is there something that you need to change within yourself, or is there something outside you that needs to be avoided or changed? Does the specific location and kind of pain have any special meaning to you? And why did the pain start now?

Seeking to understand pain can itself be therapeutic. It can turn a difficult situation into a learning and growing experience. It is, of course, difficult to understand one's pain, but it is a real problem when people do not even try. Perhaps this is why Bill Wilson, co-founder of Alcoholics Anonymous, once said, "Years ago I used to commiserate with all people who suffered. Now I commiserate only with those who suffer in ignorance, who do not understand the purpose and ultimate utility of pain." Whatever the source or meaning of pain, it represents a certain wisdom of the body and mind to defend itself and to adapt to stress or infection. Whatever the nature of the pain, it is decidedly more effective to appreciate it rather than resist it. Resistance creates additional tension and usually additional pain. Loving attention, on the other hand, can have a noticeably soothing and healing effect.

Loving one's pain

Loving one's pain is certainly easier to say than do. It seems a lot simpler to feel irritated and angry about the pain, depressed and despairing about how horrible it is, and fearful and anxious about how long it will persist. But just as easily as a person in pain can assume that life is a series of problems, this person can also be intrigued by the challenge of life as a series of adventures. Instead of fretting about the pain, the person can be curiously seeking out ways to deal with it. There is also something wonderfully healing about simply giving "positive vibrations" to pain. Although this may sound nonsense, a person in pain is usually willing to do some odd things in an effort to obtain relief. Since resisting or fighting pain is like pulling at a knot from both ends, learning to love the knot sometimes loosens its grip.

As heroes in many a fairytale have reflected, "You don't have to hate the dragon to love the princess." Likewise, you do not have to hate the pain to love the challenge it creates. This may be an important first step in learning to deal with pain most effectively.

22

Are You Continually Fatigued?

---◆---

Fatigue is a frustrating condition; not only does it affect one's physical energy, but it affects one's mental energy, too. Mental jogging becomes as difficult as physical jogging. Symptoms that commonly accompany fatigue include the inability to think clearly, sleep disturbances, constipation, apathy, depression, swollen glands and difficulty in reading.

Chronic fatigue syndrome has become one of the latest garbage-can diagnoses for various fatigue-related health problems. Some physicians think that it is caused by the Epstein-Barr virus; others think it is from the HBLV virus, and still others think that it is a mixture or "cocktail" of several viruses.

Some fatigue syndromes have nothing to do with viral infections, but could be the result of anaemia, a thyroid problem or some other disease. And some fatigue syndromes result from psychological problems, although in these cases it is difficult to determine if the psychological problem caused the fatigue or vice versa.

Fatigue can be caused by overexertion, but it can also result from under-exertion. An overstressed athlete is as likely to become as fatigued as a couch potato.

The fact that you've read this far means that you're not a total basket case. Here are some strategies to get you up on your feet again and raring to go. The strategies presented here are taken from the book *The One Minute (or so) Healer*, by Dan Ullman, M.Ph. While we present eight suggestions here, the book contains eighteen one-minute strategies for fatigue.

Energy creates energy

Exercise may sound like an impossible dream when you're fatigued, but it does stimulate circulation and metabolism. Regular exercise usually enhances energy, but be careful not to exhaust yourself.

Take a cold shower

Taking a cold shower will really wake you up ! If you are not brave enough to take one, then take a cold foot bath, or simply splash your face with cold water.

Avoid cheap tricks

Drinking coffee and eating sweets may give you short-term energy, but they can lead to greater fatigue because these substances sap the adrenal glands and disrupt blood-sugar levels. Stay away from these energy robbers.

Watch your protein

Fatigue can result from having too much protein or too little. Make certain that you are getting enough but not too much. One meal per day, maybe two at the most, should have a food item rich with protein. Meat and dairy products are sources of protein, but there are healthier alternatives. You can get complete protein meals with less fat by eating plenty of whole grains, vegetables, legumes and seeds. Herbal interferon echinacea is a herb that has been proven effective in reducing viral activity. It also stimulates the immune system, and some people with fatigue who take it have noticed improved energy and stamina. Take fifteen drops of echinacea tincture three times a day.

Consider super herbs

Ginseng and ginkgo are two powerful herbs that tend to energise people. Because these are usually expensive herbs, get standardised extracts of them so that you know precisely what and how much you are getting of the herb.

Consider super foods

Spirulina and bee pollen are nutrition-rich super foods. Some people claim that they get a big boost in energy from them. Blend one teaspoon of each into a juice, or take a couple of capsules of each with a meal.

Take your job seriously and love it

If you truly love your work, it can be the best energiser for you. Anything that gives your life purpose and meaning is highly therapeutic. If you are unable to change jobs and work at something you really feel passionate about, find something in your job that you love.

23
The Issue of Obesity

◆

"Fat is beautiful, along with every other shape, size or form. The oldest depiction of divinity on earth is the Goddess of Willendorf, a large-breasted, large-bellied clay mother-figure 30,000 years old," observes Diane Stein, author of *Natural Remedy*.

"Certainly this is good to recall when fat has become an obsession, such as with anorexia, bulimia, constant dieting and bingeing, when the issue of weight is clearly out of perspective," comments Mary Pat Palmer. "While fat is a feminist issue, it is also a health issue. Obesity can endanger the internal organs through clogging, making exercise difficult and slowing down the entire system. All of the internal organs can be endangered, particularly the heart." Obesity arises from many general places. Obesity can be hereditary, although there is some question about the behavioural component and the genetic, or it can result from a glandular disorder. Eating the "wrong foods" can contribute to obesity. Over-eating is another factor, again somewhat complicated because conditions can become habitual in the system, such as the slowing of the metabolism. People do have different metabolic rates and these play a very strong role in their body type.

Other causes

Over-eating can be programmed in early childhood. Many of the psychological components are familiar, such as the caretakers giving sweets rather than physical and/or verbal affection-rewards, displays of affection and attention coming in the form of sugar.

A very high percentage of incest survivors have eating disorders. One client feels that her body size has protected her from advances from men who are "interested only in the outside, not the inside, of a woman". Certainly weight gain can be viewed as a logical reaction to the insane advertising of our media. Unfortunately, as with many defences, it can be turned inward with harmful effects. Ironically, eating disorders are at times a defence that arises from a control issue. Over-eating can become an obsessive-compulsive problem. Many children who endure over-controlling caretakers are fighting back with an eating disorder. Eating, urinating and defecating are within their control and disorders in these realms almost always indicate over-controlling parental figures. Over-eating compulsively is a paradox. It is behaviour that is out of control but arose from a need to have control. Therapeutic input can be helpful.

Nutrition factor

Nutrition is also important. On a diet of white flour, sugar, etc., one may be filling oneself again and again searching for nutrients. Obesity factors include high fat diets, animal protein foods containing cholesterol and saturated fats, sugar, natural hormones present in milk products (particularly epidermal growth factor), natural and synthetic sex hormones added to animal feed or implanted directly into them, and a lack of exercise.

If grain is not well chewed, it can contribute to flatulence and overweight. Saliva released while chewing contains the enzyme ptyalin which initiates the breakdown of starches.

Overloading your body with food damages organs of

elimination, from the bloodstream to the kidneys. Hard-to-break-down fats, meat, dairy and "empty calories" – sugar, white flour and such – tax your body. Add to this pesticides, herbicides, synthetic hormones and other banes of civilisation and your body is working overtime and clogged. Clogging can inhibit elimination. Constipation can cause toxins to back up into the system. Flax seed and senna (with ginger added to prevent griping) help with constipation.

The benefits of herbs

Herbs can play many safe and effective roles with obesity. Louise Tenney writes in *Today's Herbal Health* that "Herbs help the body adjust as well as supply vitamins and minerals. This combination acts as a general body cleanser, regulates metabolism, dissolves fat in the body, helps eliminate craving for food, stimulates glandular secretions, reduces water retention, boosts energy and helps in constipation." An admirably inclusive statement.

The alternatives are very important for long-term use. Everyone can form a daily tea based on important alternatives such as red clover and alfalfa with other herbs added for personal taste and preference. Chickweed is the herb most often thought of for metabolising and burning fat. It also serves as an appetite depressant. It is wonderful in salads. Tinctures are preferable to the dried leaf. Diane Stein names chickweed along with cleavers and poke root as herbs that "stimulate weight loss by helping to burn fat". Susun Weed waxes eloquent about chickweed with a full chapter in her book, *Healing Wise*. Regulators such as kelp are extremely important because they are so good for the glands. Lemon balm (Melissa) would also be important for the glands due to its function in the lymph system. Diuretics can be important when

the weight appears as oedema or water gain. Da
nettle and fennel are good additions to a daily t

Diane Stein has a long list of herbs in *Natur* that includes yerba maté (which contains caffeine), hawthorn and alfalfa. She also recommends stevia as a sweetener. She uses stevia quite a lot, particularly in baking, and it has the additional advantage of being a blood-sugar regulator.

Mary Carse in *Herbs of the Earth* points out that obesity can also become a problem at menopause because of glandular changes. She recommends seaweed (sea vegetables), yarrow, prickly ash and a short fast once a month.

Holistic approach

As with most disorders, and even more than with some, obesity must be viewed holistically. Many factors can enter into this disorder, including psychological issues, heredity, behavioural training, nutrition and blockages.

One cannot simply say, "Here, take this and call me next week." It is a health problem. A big woman is not necessarily an obese woman. There are big women who radiate health and thin women who do not. We might disagree since we live in a culture where women are portrayed in advertising as pre-pubescent boys (perhaps with breasts). We can work to change this imagery. We can use herbs that help. We can remember our allies in kelp, gotu kola, chickweed, yarrow, cleavers, poke root, prickly ash, dandelion, nettle, fennel, yerba maté, hawthorn, stevia, flax seed, senna and, with caution, ephedra.

24

High Blood Pressure Disorder

◆

High blood pressure, or hypertension, is a very difficult health disorder condition for a number of reasons, writes Maureen Keane in her book, *The Red Yeast Rice Cholesterol Solution*. It is very common, affecting an estimated 24 per cent of all adults in America, for example, about 43 million people. Among older adults the percentage is even higher.

The effects of hypertension on tissues can be devastating. Not only does it accelerate atherosclerosis, but it is a leading cause of strokes, kidney disease and congestive heart failure. Worst of all, hypertension does all this damage silently. The victim feels no pain or discomfort. Typically, there are no symptoms at all. When a victim does finally experience difficulties, the disease has already severely damaged tissues and vessels. Hypertension is not a disease but a disorder. Once it is established, it changes the structure of the arterioles – the small muscular arteries. The smooth muscle cells in the arterial wall multiply and enlarge so that the walls become thicker and the opening becomes smaller. They also contract, further constricting the opening. Think of your arteries as a garden hose. When water comes out the end of the hose, it continues for an inch or two and then drops straight to the ground. You can't water that bush at the other end of the garden with just a hose. For that you need to attach a nozzle, a tube that is narrower than the hose. When the water goes through the constricted nozzle, it is under greater pressure. It shoots out the end, easily reaching your bush ten feet away. And the narrower you make your nozzle, the farther the water goes.

Aim your nozzle at the ground and it will move dirt and rocks with ease. It can also rip away part of your lawn if you are not careful. When your arteries constrict, your blood behaves like the water going through the nozzle.

If the pressure in your arteries gets high enough, it too can rip things. In this case, endothelial cells. High blood pressure can peel the lining off artery walls and otherwise inflict trauma on these delicate cells. There is no clear-cut threshold of blood pressure above which damage occurs. The detrimental effects of hypertension increase continuously as pressure increases.

Dietary recommendations for hypertension

It is very clear that diet affects blood pressure. Vegetarians, for example, tend to have lower blood pressures than non-vegetarians. When a group of people move from an area that has a low incidence of high blood pressure to one that has a high incidence of high blood pressure, they gradually assume the blood pressure incidence of the adopted area as they adopt the new diet.

Just how effective are diets in controlling blood pressure? The American Heart Association Nutrition Committee estimates that a reduction in diastolic blood pressure of just two millimetres of mercury (mm Hg) could lower a person's stroke risk by as much as 15 per cent and lower heart disease risk by 6 per cent.

Hypertension and salt

A higher intake of salt is related to higher blood pressure, and there is good evidence that certain people with hypertension can lower their blood pressure by lowering their salt intake. If you suffer from high blood pressure, ask your physician if you are salt sensitive.

Most people eat much more salt than they need, and since too much of anything is never a good idea, it is recommended that everyone consume salt in moderation. A high intake of sodium is associated with more health problems than just hypertension. For the general population, the American Heart Association recommends that the average daily consumption of salt does not exceed 6 grams. The DASH (Dietary Approaches to Stop Hypertension) diet below contains 7.5 grams in comparison to the standard American diet, which averages 10 mg. This is not difficult to achieve on a whole foods diet such as the Red Yeast Rice Diet since most salt is invisibly hidden inside processed foods. When you avoid junk foods, you also avoid excess salt.

The sodium found in salt is not the only mineral implicated in hypertension. While modern diets contain too much sodium and chloride, they also contain too little of the other electrolyte minerals such as potassium, calcium and magnesium. Several studies have shown that people who eat diets rich in potassium-containing foods tend to have lower blood pressure, while other studies have found this association in diets rich in calcium. Instead of blaming one mineral it might make more sense to consider hypertension a result of mineral imbalance.

The DASH diet

Rather than examine the effect of an individual nutrient or supplement, a group of researchers studied the impact of whole dietary patterns on blood pressure. The study group consisted of 459 adults with a starting blood pressure less than 160 mm Hg systolic and 80–95 mm

Hg diastolic. Of those, 133 had high blood pressure and 326 had normal.

For the first three weeks, volunteers ate the control diet, which was designed to imitate the average American diet. It was high in fat and low in fruits, vegetables and dairy products. They were then randomly assigned to three groups. Each diet contained the same number of calories and amount of sodium.

One group continued on the control diet.

A second group ate a modified control diet that was similar to the control diet (high in fat) but provided nine to ten servings of fruits and vegetables and fewer sweets and snacks.

A third group ate a combination diet – combination because it combined most of the characteristics that were thought to lower blood pressure. It contained less fat, saturated fat and cholesterol, nine to ten servings of fruits and vegetables and three servings of low-fat dairy foods.

After eight weeks blood pressures were again measured. When compared with the control diet, the combination diet significantly lowered both systolic and diastolic pressure while the fruit/vegetable diet lowered only systolic. The effect was apparent within one week and was at its greatest and most stable at two weeks and after. Blood pressure reduction was greater in minority subjects when compared to non-minorities, but the difference was not statistically significant.

Subjects with high blood pressure showed a greater response than those with normal pressures. Among the 326 participants with normal blood pressure, the combination diet reduced systolic pressure by 3.5 mm Hg and diastolic blood pressure by an average of 2.1 mm Hg. But in the 133 participants with high blood pressure, the combination diet reduced systolic pressure 11.4 mm Hg and diastolic blood pressure 5.5 mm Hg. These results are similar to those seen with drug therapy, and the DASH research team has stated that their combination diet may be a good alternative to drug therapy for those subjects with Stage 1 hypertension. If everyone adopted a DASH-type diet, it is estimated the incidence of coronary heart disease would fall by 15 per cent and stroke by 27 per cent! The Red Yeast Rice Diet is very similar to the combination diet. If you have hypertension and would like to duplicate the DASH diet, just add a few more servings of fruit and vegetables to the diet. Make sure your mineral supplement contains potassium.

Hypertension, stroke and potassium

Diets rich in fruits, vegetables and whole grain cereals may reduce a person's risk of stroke, especially in individuals with high blood pressure. Many researchers believe this is because the mineral content of the whole foods lowers blood pressure. A number of small studies suggested that a high intake of potassium in the diet could help reduce the risk of stroke. Researchers set out to determine whether these findings would still hold true in a larger study. They questioned 43,738 men who were part of the Health Professionals Follow-up Study, a dietary investigation of men who were free of heart disease and diabetes and who had not had a stroke. Of those, 8,520 had hypertension. During the eight-year study 328 individuals had strokes.

Individuals in the top fifth of dietary potassium intake had a 38 per cent lower risk of stroke than those in the bottom fifth. The major difference between the diets of the two groups was in their consumption of fruits and vegetables – nine servings daily in the highest potassium group compared with four in the lowest.

Individuals who had high blood pressure and who

were also taking potassium supplements (about one gram per day) reduced their risk of stroke by 60 per cent when compared to those with high blood pressure who weren't taking supplements.

Men without high blood pressure whose diets were high in magnesium and cereal fibre also had a reduced risk of stroke when compared to men who ate lower levels of these nutrients.

Those with high intakes of magnesium had a 30 per cent decreased risk of stroke and those with high intakes of cereal fibre had a 40 per cent decreased risk compared with those who ate low levels of these nutrients.

Other studies have shown that a high potassium diet may reduce high blood pressure. In this case, however, the lower incidence of stroke did not seem to be caused by lower pressures. The differences in blood pressure were too small to cause such a dramatic decrease in stroke risk. Researchers concluded that there is strong support for a stroke-preventive effect from diets rich in potassium, magnesium and cereal fibre. This was found to be particularly true in individuals with high blood pressure, further suggesting that high potassium diets might be beneficial in this segment of the population.

Diet tips for hypertension

- Choose fruits and vegetables that are rich in potassium, magnesium and calcium.

- Reduce the amount of caffeine and sugar in your diet. Both can increase the amount of potassium that is excreted by the kidney.

- Supplement your diet with a comprehensive mineral supplement that contains calcium, magnesium and potassium.

- Eat fatty fish at least twice a week and take a fish oil supplement with it.

Less salt, fewer strokes

Research has shown that the risk of having a stroke increases as blood pressure increases. Research has also shown that drug treatment can decrease the incidence of stroke. Recently a study done by St George's Hospital Medical School found that a modest reduction in salt intake was just as effective in lowering blood pressure as treatment with diuretics such as thiazides.

This English study looked at forty-seven volunteers aged sixty to seventy-eight years with a blood pressure range of 123–205 mm Hg systolic and 64–112 mm Hg diastolic. A diet low in salt (five grams a day) was compared to a diet high in salt (ten grams a day). Participants with both high blood pressure and normal pressure experienced a decrease in blood pressure. The average reduction was 7.2 mm Hg systolic and 3.2 mm Hg diastolic. This was estimated to correspond to a 36 per cent reduction in stroke risk over a five-year period!

The researchers concluded that the decrease in blood pressure achievable through a low-salt diet could result in a major reduction in the incidence of strokes. What is important is that the reduction in salt intake was accomplished simply by not cooking with salt, not adding salt at the table and avoiding salted junk foods.

How to reduce salt intake

To achieve no more than 2,400 mg/day of sodium, choose foods that are naturally low in salt, like fresh fruits and vegetables. Limit excessively salty foods: smoked, cured or processed meat; some convenience foods like frozen meals and canned soups; certain spices such as soy sauce, garlic salt and other salted condiments, highly salted snacks like salted crackers, crisps, pretzels, popcorn and nuts; and many sauce mixes and 'instant' products. Break the habit of adding salt to food or water during cooking or at the table. Use herbs, spices and fruit juices in place of salt to season food, and rinse canned vegetables to remove excess salt. Read the nutrition label on food packages to select foods lower in sodium.

25
Ayurvedic Principles and Guidelines

◆

According to Ayurvedic teaching, starting any form of treatment without first dealing with the toxins in the system that have caused the disease will only make matters worse. In the short term, treatment may superficially relieve the symptoms, but the imbalance in the doshas will manifest as disease again either in the same location or elsewhere. (Doshas refer to three energies or forces corresponding to the three basic body types in Ayurvedic medicine: vata, pitta, kapha.) Toxins may either be eliminated or neutralised. This applies to both the physical and emotional level of disease, write Angela Hope-Murray and Tony Pickup in a study which we cite below.

The emotional level

Anxiety, anger, fear, insecurity, jealousy and greed are human emotions recognised by us all, but as children we are taught that it is not appropriate to express these "negative" feelings. Ayurveda teaches us that this is incorrect thinking and that it is important to release these emotions, otherwise imbalance in the doshas will occur, leading to a build-up of disease-creating toxins.

First of all, we need to know what our repressed emotions are. Sometimes they have been so effectively buried that we are quite unaware of them. The only way to find out is through observation. This is a little more than plain observation of what is going on in our lives –

it involves observing the observer, even though that sounds almost impossible. It helps to ask the question: "Who is it that observes you are happy (or sad or angry, etc.)?" "Who is it that is aware you are seeing this page?" The answer is the true self, or the soul, unchangeable and unaffected by the exigencies of life; in Western medicine it is sometimes referred to as insight – literally looking inward.

There are many techniques to assist in this process of observation. It helps to pause for a couple of seconds before doing anything; discussion with a group of like-minded individuals refines the ability to make contact with this insight; meditation is extremely useful.

Observation is the key to understanding your emotions. For example, if anger arises, you should be completely aware of it – do not try to do anything about it, just observe it. In this way you will learn how it arose and what it resulted in. Release of anger is the important feature and, once again, this involves not doing anything; simple observation will enable its release.

The physical level
Diet

The guiding principle of Ayurveda is that each person has the power to heal herself. Much can be done to remove or neutralise toxins in the body by balancing the doshas, using an appropriate diet as part of a programme of measure in all aspects of life. Such dietary adjustments also serve to maintain the balance of the doshas and thus perfect health. Spiritual development is vitally important, but it is difficult to maintain if the body and mind are ailing, so our eating habits must be examined. What is eaten should be chosen to balance the individual constitution. Choosing the proper diet is a simple matter when given an understanding of the constitution and how it relates to the qualities of various foods. The taste of the food (sweet, sour, salty, pungent, bitter or astringent) and the season of the year must also be considered.

You should not eat unless you are feeling hungry, nor drink unless you are feeling thirsty. Do not confuse these two feelings; the temptation to drink in order to assuage hunger is great; but all that will happen is that the digestive fire will be diluted.

In the process of eating, you are feeding not just the body but the mind and spirit as well. It is important, therefore, to feed all five of the senses by preparing and consuming food that is attractive to look at, good to taste, inspiring to smell and pleasant in constitution. It may seem difficult to satisfy the sense of hearing, but the sound of food being cooked, or of a stick of raw celery being chewed, can do so in a very pleasing way.

Always prepare, serve and eat food with love. We have all had the experience that food cooked by someone who loves us is somehow more pleasing than that cooked without love. Holding on to negative feelings while we are eating tends to cause indigestion. Poor digestion will give rise to production of ama (toxic material caused by poor digestion) and thus to the promotion of disease. Drink water with your meal in sips. After you have finished eating, a mixture of yoghurt and water will aid digestion. This drink should be about half yoghurt and half water, but see what suits you best. If you have vata as a strong characteristic (light, thinly built, excitable) then add a little lemon juice. If your major dosha is pitta (medium build, precise speech and action), then add a little sugar. For kapha individuals (solid, powerful build, tranquil, relaxed), a little honey and a sprinkle of fresh black pepper is probably a good idea. This is specifically a drink for the end of, rather than during, a meal. The best drink during the meal itself is water; do not drink milk with a meal, especially if the food contains meat.

If possible, allow your food to pass through the digestive system before doing any strenuous exercise. When you exercise, the body reduces the blood supply to the gut and makes it available to the appropriate muscles; this disrupts the whole process of digestion and must be avoided if ama is not to be produced. The same is true of sleeping; the circulation of blood in the body changes profoundly and the gut is no longer supplied with what it needs to allow correct digestion and assimilation of what you have just eaten. Avoid both these "activities" for a good two hours after a meal. This does not mean that you cannot go for a stroll after eating – it is almost certainly beneficial to take a gentle walk following a meal. Food has the property, as far as digestion is concerned, of being either heavy or light, related largely to the amount of digestion required. Light foods include cooked rice and potatoes, whereas heavy foods include things like raw food and cooked meat. In the West, we tend to think that salads are "light" food, but they actually require a lot more digestion than a cooked vegetable. Raw and cooked food have different amounts of agni (digestive fire) present in them and should never be eaten in the same meal, except in very small quantities.

Light food makes it easier to integrate body, mind and spirit because there is less redistribution of blood to the gut for digestion. Heavy food always leaves you feeling tired and lethargic and often actually induces sleep.

Diet and the mind

Everything you eat will affect your mind as well as your body. In Ayurveda, the mind has three possible states that are related to the state of the constitution as a whole:

- sattva, or peaceful equilibrium, in which the power of discrimination is most accessible
- rajas, or activity, in which excessive thoughts prevent discrimination from being accessed
- tamas, or inertia, in which there is a heaviness and attachment to the physical realm such that there is neither activity nor discrimination.

This division of states of mind is the cause of another of those vicious circles that tend to characterise our lives. The power of discrimination allows us to know the correct balance and what is the most appropriate action in a certain situation. If this is clouded, or access to it is not possible, then we are unable to decide, for example, what to eat and how much; this can give rise to a more tamasic state (having the quality of tamas or inertia), which further obscures discrimination!

Food that is bad, fermented or preserved for too long increases the amount of tamas in the body and then in the mind. A good example of fermented food is alcohol. This does not mean we should not drink alcohol, but we are all aware of the effects of too much! Legumes and high-protein food like meat, fish and poultry increase rajas, as do any of the pungent spices. To increase sattva we should increase our intake of grains, fruits and vegetables.

Do's and don'ts

Always eat fresh foods when possible and avoid preserved, canned or frozen food items, though the latter are permissible if fresh is not available. Eat light foods until your appetite is satisfied, but do not be tempted to clear the plate just because there is food on it. With heavy foods, try to restrict yourself to satisfying only half your appetite with this type of ingredient. If you are ill, eat only light foods, and then in small quantities, until half your appetite – at the most – is satisfied. One of the most important rules in Ayurveda is never to combine in one meal foods that "fight", either in terms of the signals they give to the gut or in terms of their qualities:

- do not eat cooked foods and raw foods at the same meal since they require different types of digestion
- avoid combining heavy and light foods
- avoid drinking milk while eating radishes, tomatoes, potatoes, bananas, meat, fish, eggs, citrus fruits, melon, bread or cherries
- do not mix milk and yoghurt
- eat fresh fruit separately from other meals (cooked fruit may be eaten at the same time as a cooked meal)
- avoid mixing different types of protein, such as meat and cheese.

In recent years, Western medical research has identified other unhelpful food combinations in line with the traditional Ayurvedic ones above. Keep heavy high-protein or high-fat food items in separate meals from lighter foods such as starches and vegetables. These types of food require quite different digestive processes in the gut for proper nutrition. If you eat them together, there will be competition for the appropriate digestive mechanism and neither will be digested properly. Proteins and fats require slow digestion and absorption by the small bowel, whereas starches need to pass quickly to the large bowel where they are acted upon by bacteria to produce special forms of nutrients. Your small bowel needs this form of food. If they are eaten together, then fat and protein slow down the passage of the starches and they do not reach the large bowel in time to be digested by this special bacterial mechanism. It is your bowel that suffers and is unable to function properly as the controller of nutrients entering the body.

Do your best to maintain the separations between different types of foods as indicated above – there is nothing "wrong" with any of them, they just do not combine well.

26
The Sleep–Health Link in Ayurveda

According to a report by Rama Kant Mishra, on a typical day in America, 125 million people wake up feeling exhausted. "They reach to shut off the alarm clock with bleary eyes, vowing to get more sleep. But for 50 per cent of the nation's population, getting a good night's sleep is as difficult as flying to the moon."

"I have people coming into my office every day complaining of insomnia at night and fatigue during the day," says Dr Harold Bloomfield, Yale-trained physician and the best-selling author of *Healing Anxiety Naturally*. "This is an epidemic and an epidemic on the rise." Indeed, insomnia and fatigue are now considered top health problems. Researchers have identified lack of sleep as a cause of serious disorders ranging from diabetes to high stress levels. The results show that it is taking a huge toll on the quality of life – and the health – of millions. Here are some research facts that might make you head for the bed: sleep deprivation is credited with 60 per cent of road accidents – and drivers who stayed awake over seventeen hours suffered impaired coordination, reaction time and judgement worse than drivers who were legally drunk. Worker fatigue is linked to the *Challenger* disaster, the Chernobyl nuclear meltdown and the *Exxon Valdez* oil spill. As far as health goes, those who sleep fewer than six hours a night do not live as long as those who sleep seven hours or more. Sleeping only four hours a night can cause weight gain, diabetes and high blood pressure.

And the disasters are not limited to health – sleeplessness costs the US economy $150 billion a year in higher levels of worker stress and reduced productivity, estimates the National Sleep Foundation.

Stress and insomnia: a vicious cycle

What are the causes of this epidemic? One of the reasons that insomnia (defined as having trouble sleeping) is on the rise in America is the high stress levels and time pressures associated with modern living. "We are increasingly a 24–7 (twenty-four hours, seven days a week) society," says Dr Harold Bloomfield. "Many people would gladly get more sleep if they could, but the information age, which was supposed to make everything more efficient, has just made everything more busy." People frequently fall into a vicious cycle, with stress during the day causing them to be too tense or worried to fall asleep at night. And then the lack of sleep, in turn, creates more stress on the job and at home. Others simply choose to short-change their sleep. "Our society seems to place a moral value on sleeping as little as possible," says Dr Eve Van Couter, head of a recent research study at the University of Chicago. For whatever reason, people today often sleep less than six hours a night, making them highly vulnerable to sleep disorders, the stress syndrome and to multiple health problems.

Natural solutions needed

Unfortunately, most people are treating insomnia either by going to the chemist and buying over-the-counter drugs, or by consulting their medical doctor. "Neither solution is working," observes Dr Bloomfield. "Over-the-counter drugs contain antihistamines, which knock you out but don't create a good quality of sleep or solve the underlying problem. Plus, they undermine the immune system." Doctors tend to prescribe Valium-like drugs that are addictive within even a week of use. Millions are addicted to tranquillisers to reduce stress during the day and sleeping pills to induce sleep at night. "You don't induce a natural state of sleep with unnatural, synthetic and, in many cases, highly addictive, products," notes Dr Bloomfield.

Dr Bloomfield recommends that patients who suffer from insomnia restore a balanced rest/activity cycle by practising the Transcendental Meditation technique, which has been shown in a number of studies to reduce stress and insomnia. He also recommends the natural lifestyle tips and products suggested by Ayurveda, the ancient system of holistic healing from India.

The Ayurvedic approach

The goal of the Ayurvedic approach is to create more ojas – the finest product of digestion that provides energy, enthusiasm, happiness, clarity of thought, better coordination between the heart and mind, and immunity. Only the deepest, most restful sleep, called Stage 4 sleep by researchers, creates ojas. A good quality of sleep provides deeper rest to the mind and senses and enhances capacity for mental and physical work the next day. On the other hand, lack of sleep increases ama, or toxins in the body. Ayurveda identifies three types of sleep disorders.

Type 1: Difficulty falling asleep (caused by vata imbalance or mental stress). People who toss and turn, unable to fall asleep because their mind is whirling, have this disorder. It tends to correlate with anxiety, worry and rushed activity during the day.

Recommendations from Ayurveda for Type 1 imbalance:
Eat more sweet, sour and salty foods.
Eat three warm, cooked meals at the same time every day.
Get to bed before 10:00 p.m. and rise by 6:00 a.m.
Avoid rushed work hurriedly done.
Eat poppy-seed chutney one hour before bed.
Massage your hands and feet with massage oil.
Use a relaxing aroma or aroma blend at bedtime.
Drink a cup of herbal tea before bed.
Listen to some soothing music before bed.

Type 2: Intermittent awakening (caused by pitta imbalance or emotional trauma). With this disorder you fall asleep fine but wake up every 90 minutes with your heart racing, your muscles tense, and emotions of fear, anger and sadness. Or another pattern is that you wake up between 2:00 and 4:00 a.m., full of energy, and find it impossible to go back to sleep.

Recommendations:
Avoid spicy foods.
Eat more sweet, bitter and astringent tastes.
Avoid skipping meals.
Eat enough dinner so you don't wake up hungry.
Before bed, massage your feet with massage oil.
Drink a cup of relaxing or soothing herbal tea before bed.

If you wake up in the night, have a snack of half a cup of warm whole milk and 1 teaspoon rose petal jam. Roses are cooling for the mind, body and emotions.

If your head feels hot when you wake up in the night, mix three tablespoons of coconut oil with five drops of lavender oil and massage it on the crown of your head.

Type 3: Sleeping long hours but waking up unrefreshed (caused by kapha imbalance). Sometimes it's an early-morning awakening, sometimes it's characterised by sleeping in, but in any case, you will feel sluggish, tired and completely exhausted even though you've had a full night's sleep.

Recommendations:
Be sure to rise before 6:00 a.m.
Do a morning massage with warm massage oil.
Exercise every day.
Sip warm water throughout the day.
Avoid eating too many heavy, sweet, sour and salty foods.
Eat a light, warm dinner (soup is ideal) and season the food with fresh ginger and a small amount of black pepper.
Drink a cup of relaxing herbal tea before bedtime.

Some Ayurvedic herbs, such as muskroot and Indian valerian, are pro-sedative, meaning that they help a person to relax into sleep. A large number of research studies show that Indian valerian induces sleep. Other herbs, such as brahrni and ashwagandha, restore the body's own inner intelligence to improve the quality of sleep. A third group of herbs helps to slowly repair any damage resulting from prolonged sleep problems, such as damage to the immune system and weakened coordination between heart and mind. Due to the synergistic combination of a variety of herbs, there are no side-effects. There is no groggy feeling (as created by modern drugs and by some single-ingredient natural remedies), but instead people report a fresh feeling of enthusiasm, increased ability to concentrate, reduced stress and better managing ability.

Going to bed earlier

For all three types of imbalance, it is recommended that you fall asleep before 10:00 p.m. That is because after 10:00, a more active, pitta-quality sleep sets in. If you fall asleep before then, you will imbibe more slow, restful, kapha qualities. The quality of your sleep will be deeper and you will find it easier to fall asleep. Almost anyone can experience deep, restful, Stage 4 sleep by just doing this one thing – going to bed before 10:00 p.m.

Many of these recommendations are substantiated by research. Sleep researchers, for instance, have documented that a brief period of moderate exercise three to four hours before bed, such as taking a brisk walk after dinner, can really help deepen sleep. Other studies link physical fitness with improved sleep quality.

Creating a timeless bedroom

Dr Bloomfield suggests that his patients create a "timeless bedroom". Keep time pressures away from your sleeping place. If you have to use an alarm clock, put it in a place where you cannot see it. Preserve your bedroom as a comfortable, relaxing haven, a place for warm, intimate and relaxing relationships. Keep heated discussions, intense brainstorming, television-watching, computer work and monthly budgets out of your bedroom.

Especially avoid violent, suspenseful TV shows before bed, he says. Instead, surround yourself with influences that cultivate your peace of mind while you fall asleep. Before bed take pleasant breaths: use aroma therapy or lavender to allow the relaxing scents to go directly to your olfactory lobe and help to induce sleep, sometimes within minutes.

To relax your neck and shoulders, your back and abdomen, you can do some simple, light yoga postures, and can also add very soothing music, bedtime prayers and positive affirmations to really move in the direction of being more and more peaceful.

"If you're going to be thinking of something, think of your fondest memories, particularly of childhood, where you had soothing, blissful, wonderful sleep, or when you had an amazingly restful vacation," says Dr Bloomfield. "Think of those thoughts instead of ones that cause you worry and anxiety."

What is your sleep IQ?

Even if you don't have insomnia, you might not be getting enough sleep at night. In assessing your sleep health, Dr Bloomfield suggests that you also look at how you feel during the day. If you answer "yes" to a majority of the following questions, it might be a cue that your stress levels are too high and you are not sleeping enough, or deeply enough, for your health.

- Do you have symptoms such as dullness, poor muscle tone, a lack of spontaneity?
- Do you have a tendency to be bored or depressed?
- Or on the other hand do you have tension, fear and anxiety?
- Do you suffer from decreased cooperativeness, loss of acceptance of constructive criticism, irritability, temper outbursts, lowered attention span, impaired recent memory, decreased sex drive, physical complaints such as headache or backache, decreased interest in personal care?
- Are you addicted to coffee, cigarettes, stimulants, or even alcohol or drugs?
- Are you noticing a reduction in general health and joy in living?

27

Uses of Reflexology

♦

You may ask: "How can it be that a therapy that works only on the feet (or hands) can claim to affect the whole body? Surely if I have something wrong with my feet, I might visit a reflexologist/acupressurist, but how could they help with my asthma or irritable bowel syndrome?" That it does help is illustrated by the number of people who leave their reflexologist after a course of treatment experiencing permanent relief from the problems that caused them to seek help in the first place, writes Rosalind Oxenford.

Reflexology or acupressure, she says, can provide relief because the whole body is represented on the feet and hands through points that can be individually stimulated to produce a reaction in the corresponding body part. "If I am having a consultation with someone who has a stiff and painful left shoulder following a sports injury, it is not unusual for them to remark, as I work the corresponding part on the foot, that they feel a sensation of immediate relief in their shoulder."

The flow of energy around the body

How can there be a link between the two parts? This happens because the body is linked by energy flowing along certain pathways. When stimulation is applied on one point along the line, it will travel along and around that line until it has travelled through every part of the body that lies in its pathway. When an impulse travels along a line, it will stimulate everything that lies in its path. Organs and body parts that are functioning well will allow energy to flow through freely with little change. When the impulse meets a damaged area, however, the physiological effect of the increased flow of energy will be to stimulate that part to heal itself. Imagine a stream travelling along its path. Where it is clear the stream will run along freely, covering the miles effortlessly. But if it should meet boulders in its path, or a fallen tree, the water will be restricted and will push and squeeze its way through the constricted area. It will work gradually to clear the path of congestion so that it can proceed more fully. Or imagine an electrical circuit. Energy will always keep flowing, it will pass through things – or around things if they do not conduct electricity – but it cannot stop and disappear. Just as your blood travels around your body and flows without ceasing while you are alive, so electromagnetic energy flows constantly through our bodies, writes Oxenford.

This has not yet been fully explained or understood in relation to the human body, she asserts, yet it is a clearly explained and central part of physics. (Physics is the study of natural science and particularly of the properties – other than chemical – of matter and energy.) We are part of the natural world, and are indisputably composed of matter and energy. Therefore it seems probable that we will soon understand energy much more fully. Indeed, research has and is being carried out that has already increased our understanding of these matters. In 1628, when it was first suggested by William Harvey that the blood circulated around our bodies, the idea was received incredulously and the theory treated as heretical. We seem to be going through much the same process today with regard to the energy in our bodies.

Why reflex points? What is a reflex?

Most of us are familiar with the knee-jerk reflex that doctors use to test our reactions. This involves a circuit in the nervous system that travels to the spinal cord and back without involving the brain. The reflexes on the feet do not work through this very simple process. It has not yet been fully explained what the reflexes of reflexology are (they are linked with the flow of energy around the body and will no doubt be better understood when both are further researched), but we do know how the reflexes work. We know that pressure applied to the foot produces a mirrored response in the body, and that the response will be found in specific parts according to the specific points of the foot that have been touched. The link between these corresponding parts seems to be through energy, rather than through a direct material link.

Therapy given with the hands

Treatment is given with the hands using pressure techniques, the fingers applying specific pressure to areas that are sometimes very small points. A reflexology treatment consists of stimulation to specific points given within a foot massage. Reflexology is not foot massage, which is a relaxing, whole-hand massage technique applied to the feet to stimulate and generally relax the body. Reflexology uses foot massage to prepare and relax the feet for specific pressure techniques that are precisely aimed to correspond to individual organs or body parts.

The body is mirrored on the feet

The side view of the human form corresponds closely to the side view of the foot. The curves of the spine are exactly mirrored in the curves around the bony structure of the foot. The two feet together roughly represent the human torso. The spine runs down the centre of the instep of each foot where the centre of the body lies. The head and neck are represented on the toes and the neck of the toes: the big toe represents the whole head, with fine tuning for the eyes, ears, neck and teeth found on the smaller toes. The ball of the foot is the chest area bounded by the diaphragm. The abdomen lies in the instep and the pelvic area is all around the heel.

The limbs do not feature much on the feet. The limbs are superimposed on to other areas. When you have a specific problem on a limb, for instance tennis elbow, you would work the arm area on the foot, but you would also work that area on the matching limb. Therefore for someone with tennis elbow in their right arm you would work the corresponding joint on the right leg, which is the knee. These reflexes found on the limbs are referred to as cross reflexes (working across from one limb to the other on the same side).

In this way, all the various parts of the body fit on to the feet – the left and right feet mirroring the left and right sides of the body. Wherever there is illness in the body we can find a corresponding area in the foot that may be tender or painful, and where waste materials have collected in the form of deposits. Reflexology works by massaging the feet to break down these deposits, dispersing the pain and restoring the energy flow to a state of balance. Tension is relaxed throughout the muscles and the nervous system and circulation is increased, releasing or reducing the strain from which the body is suffering.

How reflexology affects the body

When the energy is flowing freely around your body you are physically, mentally and emotionally well-balanced and in harmony with your environment. The functioning of the organs is improved by releasing tension held in the body. Muscles control the workings of the organs (each tiny hair on your skin has its own muscles, for example, and your digestive system can only function through its own set of muscles) as well as large movements of the body through activity of the limbs. Treatment stimulates the circulation of the blood and lymph so that the removal of waste products and toxins is increased and the supply of nutrients throughout the blood supply is improved. By releasing long-term muscular contractions the constrictions they have imposed on the nerves are relieved and the nerve supply is freed. These are the physiological effects of reflexology treatment.

What does it feel like?

Patients receiving reflexology treatment often feel tenderness as certain points are worked, and they usually experience an immediate release of tensions (some will experience an initial reaction or healing crisis). This can be seen as well as felt when a person who comes in tired and depleted changes his whole attitude with the relaxing of tension. A glow of vitality can be seen as the energy flow begins to restore balance and wellbeing.

The number of treatments needed varies according to the type of disorder and the length of time it has been suffered. Usually the trouble yields more quickly when it is of recent origin. When a great deal of repair and healing is needed, the time required for recovery is longer.

Reflexology is an ideal way of treating children. They invariably enjoy it and it is non-invasive (therefore not threatening). It is also very effective. But the pressure used must be much lighter than for adults. Babies, too, can be treated by an experienced reflexologist who knows how to adapt the pressure: for a very young baby just a few weeks old it is sufficient to stroke gently the points on the feet with one finger. The results will be immediately apparent.

28
Handling Asthma

◆

Asthma is primarily an allergic condition that can be triggered by various foods, preservatives, pollens, weeds, grasses, chemicals and fumes, the house dust mite, or tobacco. Emotional stress and vigorous exercise can also trigger an attack. Just a couple of decades ago, few people died from asthma. However, deaths in children from asthma are growing at an alarming rate. One can't help but wonder if the powerful steroidal drugs that are used to control symptoms and that also suppress the immune function play an important role in this death toll. Do not let this type of drug abuse hurt your family. Seek out alternatives. It is a matter of life and breath.

Having your breath taken away as the result of a romantic interlude is wonderful. However, if you are having your breath taken away at other times, too, consider the following strategies:

Don't just sit there, relax!

Feeling tense and anxious makes breathing more difficult. Being tense is like trying to untie a knot by pulling at both ends. Relax and the knot almost unties itself. Progressive relaxation in which you first tense and then relax muscle groups is an effective way to achieve a heightened state of relaxation. Make sure to relax those shoulders; it's hard to breathe fully when your shoulders are up around your ears (it makes hearing more difficult too).

Don't just sit there, move!

Certain exercises that strengthen the lungs can be very helpful. Swimming is best, especially the breaststroke. Aerobic dancing has also been found to be helpful to asthmatics. Start all exercise programmes slowly, take breaks when you feel a need for them and don't overdo it. There were five gold-medallists in the 1972 Olympics who suffered from asthma, so don't assume that asthma has to limit your ability to exercise.

Vacuum-cleaning therapy

Perhaps the most common substance to trigger asthmatic breathing is the faeces from the house dust mite. Vacuum as much as possible. Make certain to also vacuum the bed (and wash your pillows), since they can be perfect breeding grounds for dust mites. When you vacuum rigorously, it can become an aerobic exercise, which in itself is therapeutic. If, however, you are hypersensitive to dust, any type of vacuuming can trigger symptoms. In that case, it is best recommended to have others do "vacuum therapy" while you sit back and practise relaxation therapy.

Give your skin the brush-off

Your skin is a third lung. It breathes and oxygenates you. Avoid covering your body with oil when you have respiratory problems, since you want to keep your third lung breathing freely. Take any soft bristle brush and stimulate your skin.

Be cool

This one is easy... turn the heat down. Many people with asthma have difficulty breathing in a heated room. Open a window too, unless you are chilled by it; you will want to avoid overly cold temperatures because extremes of temperature can aggravate symptoms.

Humidify yourself

Humidifiers can help loosen the mucus that is blocking your breathing. You can help the action of the humidifier by placing a teaspoon of eucalyptus, mullein or thyme in a cold mist humidifier or vaporiser. Make sure to wash the humidifier after each use. If you do not have a humidifier, put the oil into a pot of steaming water and place your face over the pot while you cover your head with a towel. Do this for as long as it feels good.

Preserve yourself by avoiding preservatives

Certain preservatives, particularly sulphites and MSG, can trigger an asthma attack. Sulphites are often put in wine, beer, dried fruit and seafood. They are also put in salad bars to keep the vegetables looking fresh. MSG is a common ingredient in Chinese food. Ask to have your food prepared without it.

Breathergising I

Diaphragmatic breathing exercises your lungs and abdomen and helps give you a full breath. To make certain that you are doing it correctly, follow these instructions. Place your hands on your waist above the hips. Your fingers should slightly extend over the sides of your lower abdomen, and the thumb should slightly extend over the sides of your back. Focus your attention on how your hands move when you breathe. Proper diaphragmatic breathing is occurring when your hands are thrust out to each side, rather than primarily thrust forward.

Breathergising 2

Practise expiratory breathing. This type of breathing is when you inspire normally but exert slightly additional pressure during the exhalation. Do not push too hard. This breathing helps to dilate the bronchial passages. Do whatever visualisation practices will augment this breathing exercise. For instance, imagine yourself pushing out the walls of a room. This may then give you more "room for breathing".

Breathergising 3

Take a full breath through your nose. When you exhale, pronounce out loud the syllables "woo", "lee" and "ah" on separate exhalations. Pronounce each syllable for five or six seconds each. Gradually increase the length of your exhalations. After doing each syllable at least twice, observe your breath and see if you are now taking deeper, fuller breaths.

Bolster your breathing

Lie on the floor and place a bolster or large pillow under your upper back, just below the shoulders. Your head should touch the floor. Slowly place your arms above your head; your chest will be lifted and your back will be arched. Breathe fully into your chest and abdomen. Maintain this position for one to five minutes, but don't overstrain.

Do the cobra

The cobra is a yoga posture that aids asthma sufferers by opening their breathing passages. You begin by lying on your abdomen and placing your hands palms down under your shoulders. While inhaling, raise your head and then your chest, using your back muscles and your hands to support you. Try to raise yourself near the point at which your arms are not bent. Hold this position until you wish to exhale and then slowly relax yourself back to the floor. Repeat this exercise at least five times.

Your lungs are in your hands

There is an acupressure point right in your hands that will provide healing energy to the lungs. It is in the web of your hands between the thumb and first finger. You may notice that this area is very sensitive to pressure; this is a sign that it needs to be pressed. Do so for at least five seconds and repeat it several times. Another good acupressure point to improve lung function is the web between your big toe and your second toe.

Supplement your breathing

Research has shown that 100-150 mg of vitamin B6 is helpful to people with asthma. You might also want to add to this supplement with 1,000 mg of vitamin C, 200–400 IU of vitamin E and 1–4 mcg of B12 (the latter is especially good for sulphite-sensitive people).

Put spice in your life

Various pungent foods and spices have bronchodilating effects that can relieve symptoms of allergy. Of specific value are onions, garlic, chilli-peppers, horseradish and mustard.

It is coffee time

Coffee also has bronchodilating effects. Research has shown that two cups of ground coffee can relieve symptoms of asthma in one or two hours for up to six hours. Although the medicinal use of coffee may seem surprising to some people involved in natural medicine, we must remember that coffee, like every other herb, can be therapeutic in one dose and poisonous in another. Do not use this strategy if you are sensitive to coffee's other effects.

Is it a drug or is it a herb?

Ephedrine is a very popular drug that was once commonly given to people with asthma. Although this drug improves breathing, its consumption also has various side-effects, including nervousness, insomnia, increased heart beat and dizziness. Because of this, it is not as popular as it previously was. However, there is a herb called ephedra (also called ma huang and Mormon tea) which contains ephedrine in smaller, safer doses. Making a tea of ephedra with a half ounce of the branches in one pint of water and drinking one or two cups provides the benefits of ephedrine without the side-effects. You can also consider taking this herb in pill form. It should, however, be taken on a short-term basis only; and should not be taken by people with high blood pressure, insomnia, anxiety and restlessness, or prostate cancer.

Use a hair of the mite that bit you

Asthma is commonly the result of exposure to the house dust-mite, a microscopic organism that grows on house dust. This is actually one of the most common allergens in the world, and some excellent research has shown that homeopathic doses of it (the thirtieth potency) are very effective in providing relief. Consider using it every four hours for no more than a couple of days at a time. Consider seeking professional homeopathic care for a "constitutional remedy" to potentially cure the underlying allergic condition, of which the asthma is but one part.

No smothering allowed

We all sometimes feel crowded, either physically or psychologically. While this does not bother some people, it can truly suffocate others. As they say in California: "Encourage others to respect your space." In other words, kindly tell people to avoid crowding you, either physically or with their expectations. At the same time, you might explore those characteristics in yourself that seek approval from others, that desire attention and that want to be smothered by others.

Write on!

Recent research has found that keeping a journal and writing about your asthma symptoms provides therapeutic benefit, as compared with people who simply write about the mundane activities that they plan to do during the day.

Emotions allowed

Many people with asthma notice that attacks may be triggered when they bottle up their emotions. Allow yourself to feel whatever emotions you feel. Accept them and express them. The more they are bottled up inside you, the more they explode internally. Suppression of emotions can be enough to take your breath away.

Avoid cockroaches and chocolate

People with asthma are often allergic to cockroaches. Keep your house as clean as possible to discourage cockroaches from hanging around. Also, did you know that the American Food and Drink Agency allows manufacturers a certain percentage by weight of cockroach parts in chocolate? It is apparently very difficult to keep these insects out of the chocolate vats (can you blame them?), so the best way to avoid cockroaches is to avoid chocolate. Strange, but true!

29

Dealing with Acne Holistically

It has been said: "Adolescence is just one big walking pimple." Although acne is an all-too-common problem for teenagers, adults experience it as well. Acne is one of those conditions that is not physically painful or even physically discomforting; however, it certainly is a blow to the ego. Acne can turn a pretty face into a battlefield, where it looks as though bombs have exploded, soldiers are bleeding and no side is winning. It is easy to feel that acne is nature's revenge against the beauty of adolescence.

The good news is that you will grow out of acne. Most people do!

For those adults who have acne, it can be even more embarrassing than for adolescents. Here again the silver lining is that people may think that you are a teenager!

On a more serious note, it is important to realise that skin symptoms do not necessarily indicate a skin disease. Skin symptoms are most likely internal problems that are manifesting on the skin. The skin is considered the third kidney – it is another organ of elimination that the body deploys to externalise oils and other matter not excreted from the body in the urine or stools. Because acne is more of an internal problem, it manifests through external symptoms, so it is not enough to simply wash your face regularly. Treating skin problems is an inside job. Furthermore, you should be careful applying the various conventional external acne medications, for they can irritate the skin and suppress the external symptoms and create more serious internal ones. Try these strategies:

Clean up your acne

Hygiene is important and you can benefit from washing your face two or three times a day. However, more frequent scrubbing can wash away important oils from the skin that help to lubricate it. If you use makeup, make certain to wash it off every night.

Too clean is too much

Avoid using soaps that dry out the skin or that cause any redness. Do not use alcohol as an astringent because it tends to dry out your skin too much. Witch hazel solutions are more effective astringents.

A herbal wash

Take the tincture of myrrh, dilute it in a small bowl of water and use a swab of cotton to wipe your face. Myrrh's antiseptic and astringent properties can both treat and prevent acne.

Naturally antiseptic and drying

Tea tree oil is a powerful natural antiseptic and drying agent. Apply it directly to the skin wherever it is oily or where there are pimples. However, some people could be allergic to such a herbal remedy, hence it would be better to do a small patch test first. It is recommended that you use products with 15 per cent tea tree oil.

Steam those pimples out

Give yourself a facial steam-bath. Place chamomile flowers or sage leaves in a bowl of water that has just finished boiling and spread a towel over your head, thus creating a mini steam-bath for your face. If you feel you need a stronger herbal steam-bath, use tea tree oil, but be careful about using too much of this powerful, natural antiseptic (an alternative to using this herb in a steam-bath is to apply tea tree oil directly to the acne).

Oil's well does not always end well

Avoid oil-based cosmetics because they tend to clog skin pores. Cosmetic-induced acne is a common problem with many women. Look for cosmetics labelled "non-comodegenic".

Your hair carries infection

Keep hair off your face with a comb or brush. Wash your hair at least every second or third day.

To squeeze or not to squeeze

Pimples should generally not be squeezed because a pimple is an inflammation and you can bring about infection by breaking it open. Worse still, squeezing them can leave a scar on your face. However, if you are desperate and want at least some temporary improvement in your facial skin, use a hot, clean cloth or tissue to soften the pimple. This will allow you to break the pimple open with gentle pressure – the more pressure you have to use, the more likely you are to damage facial skin.

Supplement yourself

Vitamin A (25,000 IU daily), vitamin B complex (100 mg, 3 times/day), vitamin E (200–400 IU daily) and zinc (30–60 mg daily) are worthwhile supplements. Vitamin A can be used in an ointment, cream or pill.

Good fats

Essential fatty acids (flaxseed oil, evening primrose oil and borage oil are excellent sources) help keep skin soft and smooth and can dissolve fatty deposits that block skin pores. Take essential fatty acids daily.

Avoid drug abuse

Several prescription drugs, including many types of contraceptive pills and corticosteroids, can cause or aggravate acne.

Garbage inside, garbage outside

Acne can be brought about by the food you eat. Although no foods have been proven to cause acne in all sufferers, some people observe reactions to milk products, nuts, fats, fried and oily foods and chocolate.

Emotional garbage inside and outside

Emotions may be eating at you, literally. Emotional turmoil can disturb the digestive and endocrine functions, leading to inefficient digestion of oils and to a potential increase in skin oils. The first step to deal with any emotional problem is to acknowledge it. Don't deny these emotions; do not let them get the better of you either. Next, express what you are feeling; don't suppress it.

Face relaxation

Research has shown that people with acne have higher levels of anxiety and anger than other people do. However, this research did not discern if the anxiety and anger led to the acne, or if the acne led to anxiety and anger. In any case, it is worthwhile doing something so that these emotions do not take a more serious toll on your health or on your face. Relaxation exercises may help you take greater control of your anxiety and irritability, rather than vice versa. Consider meditation, progressive relaxation, breathing exercises or yoga. But don't try to do all these at the same time, since such efforts will lead to even more anxiety!

30
Healing through Aura

◆

For over twenty years, Trudy Lanitis has been involved in various forms of alternative healing as a serious student, teacher and healer. She has developed her unique Bio-Etheric Healing method over the past six years to overcome the debilitating ailments of Lyme disease and rheumatoid arthritis. Currently, Lanitis holds individual counselling sessions and conducts workshops in Bio-Etheric Healing for healing professionals and others interested in spiritual healing. Most of her work takes place around St Petersburg, Florida, and near her workspace in Kingston, New York. Bio-Etheric Healing, she says, is an innovative method of alternative healing which uses a set of communication skills based on thought processes to direct our etheric body, and through it, our full energy field (our aura) to help in healing work. It is possible to have this communication directly with one's own energy field. Also, when working with a client, a Bio-Etheric Healing professional can use this method to mobilise the client's own energy field to help in his healing. The actual healing work is not limited to face-to-face physical proximity. Rather, Bio-Etheric Healing via thought process communication can be accomplished over great distances.

This communication, and the healing work itself, is possible because of the energy field which surrounds our bodies, and indeed surrounds everyone and everything on this planet. It is called the auric field, and our own

individual envelope of this energy which su
bodies is called our aura. The first layer
closest to our physical bodies, is the etheric
plays a major role in Bio-Etheric Healing.

In almost all cases, the actual healing itself begins at the etheric body level. It is primarily with the etheric body that we communicate with thought messages to provide it the directions for healing. It is in a sense the "supervisor" of the process. The etheric body then communicates with the other participants and enlists their help, as needed, to accomplish the healing. These other players include the physical body, the brain, the other layers of the aura and the chakra system. Each of these have special functions in the healing process and the appropriate one must be called upon by the etheric body to aid in the process. The chakra system is a major player because of its unique role as the distribution system for energy flow throughout the body. However, even though the etheric body may know what is wrong and what needs healing, it won't act unless told to do so. The key to Bio-Etheric Healing is that we ourselves, or a healer, must give the etheric body directions as to what to do and it will do it.

When the etheric body is asked to heal something, it does the best it is able to do, with the information it has. The more information provided to the etheric body and the greater the accuracy of the information, the better it can accomplish its healing role.

Make friends with your etheric body – it will work miracles for you. One of life's greatest rewards is to have control over your body and to have the power and ability to stay well, and if you do become ill, to have the knowledge that may help you to heal yourself. It is sincerely hoped that what I have learned in my own personal experiences will provide you with new knowledge and tools which may help you to heal yourself and others.

Lanitis says, "I do realise that what we are talking about is working through a dimension that is not visible, yet very much there and available. It is the invisible part or dimension of yourself called the aura, and its first layer, the etheric body. Yes, it is possible! Yes, it is a reality! Yes, you can do it! For some of you it will require more faith than you now possess, but faith will come with success and with knowledge, perhaps an opening to a new awareness."

Most diseases or sicknesses start at this etheric level, she claims and most healing starts there also. Knowing this, and trusting it, is the first step to a great adventure. It is your relationship with the unseen part of yourself that is still you.

Your etheric body wants to do anything it can to help keep you healthy. It also has the ability to listen to you and to do your healing for you. At first, you may give your etheric body directions only to be amazed that it will actually do what you want it to do. Later on, if you have learned to trust your inner voice, she says, you may get a "ping", meaning "I am here," and a voice in thought form. Your etheric body is many lives older than you and can communicate with a very fine vocabulary through the use of the thought process. Furthermore, since it has a voice and does not get much chance to use it, it is delighted to have someone with whom to communicate. (Lanitis claims she had one experience, working with the etheric body of a friend, over distance, whereby her etheric body kept talking to her and asking her questions just to keep her talking to it. Later, this same friend decided to speak to her etheric body herself and was so startled when she got an answer that she stopped and didn't try it again for some time.)

As you learn to work with your etheric body, Lanitis affirms, and branch out to reach other people's etheric bodies, you will find the etheric body has a personality.

Sometimes it is very shy and you have to be very gentle with it to get it to respond. Sometimes it is very warm and friendly and eager to have a chance to use its voice. If you reach a particular etheric body more than once, it will remember you and usually greet you very warmly. It doesn't get much of a chance to talk to people, and really enjoys the contact and looks forward to it. It is wonderful to make a connection with the etheric body of another and be greeted as an old friend! "Howdee! How are you all?" "Hi, Lady," from a two-year-old that Lanitis had worked with when he was just born!

The etheric body interacts with the physical body as well as with the rest of the aura. The etheric body is able to help with most of the healing work by itself but does work with the physical body, as well as the rest of the aura as needed. When you ask it to do healing, it will usually engage the help of the physical body and other layers of the aura. There are some situations where, if you know that other layers of the aura are involved, it is best if you can identify them for the etheric body. This is especially true if you want it to use the mental, emotional, etheric template, or ketheric template layers of the aura in the healing. Therefore, when you know what specific layers of the aura are needed to help with a particular problem, it is best to tell the etheric body to call upon that specific layer for work as necessary.

If you tell it to do something, it never says, "I'll do it." It will say, "I'll try; I'll work on it," or something to that effect. The connection with you is something new for it, being as well as new for you, and it has not had the experience to know what it can or cannot do. The etheric body cannot programme itself or it would do so. You have to direct it. For example, the etheric body works with the chakra system to relieve pain. The etheric body does not feel pain itself. If you have pain, you have to tell the etheric body that you have pain and where it is exactly.

Say to the etheric body, via your thoughts, "Please break up the blocked energy causing that pain. Thank you very much." Finish by saying "Goodbye", to break the connection. It will try the utmost to help you by working with the chakra system to do so.

The mental body is involved for work with the brain and thought processes and the release of traumas. Also, the mental body is involved in obsessive behaviour. The emotional body is involved with psychological work. It is necessary to use the emotional body to get rid of simple anxiety and fear in our current life.

The seventh layer of the aura, the ketheric template layer, is used for reference when one needs to make structural changes. It has a template for everything in the physical body. One can ask the etheric body to use the information as a blueprint of a healthy body in order to know how to repair any damage, or to repair and create new cells that are damaged or missing.

Under the direction of the etheric body, the physical body can become a wondrous chemical plant. It has the ability to take the information you provide via the etheric body and use chemicals present in the body to produce the same medications that the body needs to help in healing. It produces these in the amounts necessary for your body's needs so that your body never receives dangerous doses of chemicals that might hurt it.

Once, having read that hyaluronic acid is used to offset the pain and stiffness of crippling arthritis, Lanitis asked her etheric body to produce hyaluronic acid for her, and it did. "How do I know that it did? I have the ability (and will teach you also) to speak to my etheric body and find out what's going on. Also, the pain in my knees eased up. It seems just a few drops of that acid was necessary to do the job. My body handled that without any problem. Interestingly, months after I had asked my etheric body to produce hyaluronic acid, one day my knees were particularly painful and I decided to ask my etheric body to lubricate my knees. I had forgotten about hyaluronic acid. I asked, 'What are you going to use to lubricate my knees?' My etheric body answered in a very low voice, 'Hyaluronic acid'. It was incredible!"

Here are only some examples of what the etheric body may help do for you, to give you some idea of the kind of communications you can have with it.

- You can ask questions of your own etheric body to help you to know what needs to be healed. It will know what organs or chakras are damaged or need to be worked on. Yet it will not do the work unless you tell it to do so.
- You can ask the etheric body of another person the same questions and also receive answers.
- You can ask the etheric body to stop you from grinding your teeth at night.
- Much pain is caused by blocked energy in the chakra system and it may knock out or dissolve the blocked energy in minutes if you tell it to. You must give the location of the pain or chakra involved.
- It may strengthen muscles and organs of the body. Just tell it what to do.
- It can help knock out a cold, the flu or other infections quickly; possibly overnight if the illness is caught early enough. Healing possibilities include infections, whether bacterial or viral.
- You can ask the etheric body to ward off infections, bacterial or viral. You might even ask this on a daily basis which would be especially important for people in new situations, where they have not established resistance to new germs, or for people that are being exposed to new germs because of their work. This is also very important for small children going to nursery

school or elementary school who are continuously contracting infections that they are exposed to.

Your etheric body would like to take time to get to know you, and for you to get to know it. It would love just to talk to you for a while and, if you have the time, you might want to spend some making friends with it. To do this, you need to develop your communication skills.

Communication skills

The Bio-Etheric Healing method depends on your ability to communicate on a thought level with the etheric body, either your own or someone else's. When communicating with the etheric body of someone else, distance does not matter. Also, it is these same communication skills you will sometimes need to reach and get responses from the entities in charge of the lower life forms which are involved in certain ailments.

Centring – the necessary first step

Decide in advance which energy source (for example, the etheric body) you are asking to speak to and plan exactly what you want to say. You need to physically be where you will not be disturbed. You need complete concentration. Get all extraneous thoughts out of your head and allow your body and mind to relax. Some deep breathing exercises may help to achieve this relaxation.

- Sit a short while and take deep breaths to relax. Then ask your physical body, via thought, to become centred; see how it feels.
- Sit for a few minutes with the tip of your tongue on the roof of your mouth.
- Hold your hands at your side, raise hands up from the elbows with the palms facing each other. Then

bring hands together slowly feeling the energy field of the aura between the hands until they touch in the centre of the body. Then raise both hands up to your face with hands touching each other in a prayer position and lower hands slowly until they separate about waist level. Repeat as necessary until you experience a feeling of complete calm. You are now centred.

Communication via thought processes (inner speaking/inner listening)

"When I speak of talking with the etheric body and having it answer, this all takes place in thought form. We can actually hear a voice in our heads as a response (as we sometimes hear when daydreaming). This is a thought process, or thought form response, and though it is not audible in the sense that we cannot tape it, it is clearly a voice response heard in thought form. It is the voice of our etheric body which is responding to our thought form communication. Also, even though the voice cannot be heard outside of our own inner listening, it will have its own individual characteristics and will embody the 'personality' of the etheric body which is speaking. Some voices are very low and tentative and others are strong and clear. My etheric body, for example, comes through very strong, particularly now that we are such good friends."

Some of your energy sources will answer in thought form with simple "yes" or "no" answers, but others may come across in thought form with whole sentences and have a rich vocabulary using words not in your everyday speech patterns. Responses may also come in visual image form or symbols and utilising colour.

Using thought processes is the most subtle form of

communication and may require more practice than the other methods to feel comfortable. Yet the rewards are many. You will be able to get much more complete information and you will be quite amazed at the intelligence of your contact. "My etheric body has told me," Lanitis discloses, "that she prefers to communicate with words (mentally), but that she can do it in all ways. Most of my work has been communicating with my etheric body via thought processes. By now, we are old friends. Our relationship has grown. Now we are able to converse quite easily. Sometimes my etheric body will give me information about itself that I haven't asked for, such as, 'Your skin cancer cells are now gone from your etheric self.' I was very pleased to hear that, I can assure you! It meant they would be out of my physical body soon, as well. When I first started talking to my etheric body, she would say, 'I will try,' or 'I don't know if I can do it, but I will try.' Don't forget that this is as new to your etheric body as it is to you. And it doesn't quite know what it is capable of doing, yet it will try its utmost to do what is asked. It will also, by itself, engage other layers of the aura, whenever that is needed, to help in its healing work."

Your etheric body is happy to do whatever it can to make you well. It has a mind of its own as well, but needs to be directed. It welcomes your suggestions. It also enjoys communicating with people, even others besides yourself. "When I talked to my son's etheric body in Texas (I'm in New York State), it said to me 'I really enjoy talking to you. It gives me a chance to use my voice, which I don't get to do very often.'"

Two-way communication via thought processes is accomplished via several steps such as these:

- Have the information you want and the questions you want to ask worked out as much in advance as possible.

- Find a quiet place and time when you will not be interrupted.
- Get into a meditative, inward mood, clearing your mind of all extraneous thoughts. Then get centred.
- In this centred state, contact your etheric body by phrasing the message in thought form, I wish to speak to my etheric body.
- There may be some form of acknowledgement, but not always, so be prepared for any such clue in any form, such as a "feeling", a "ping", or some visual effects. If no acknowledgement is received, assume contact and move forward to ask your first question. As above, phrase the question in your mind, in thought form, and address it to your etheric body. Await an answer. It will come to you as a mental message forming in your mind and making itself heard by you in this thought form. (It is not unlike the conversations we have while in a daydream.) Although responses will usually be in this thought form method, some people have experienced responses in visual form, such as symbols or colour. For example, a stop sign or a red light to mean "no" and a green light to mean "yes". So be prepared! Then, wait a short while for the etheric body to get ready before continuing to ask each question you have prepared. You may find it necessary to follow up each response further to explore your problem or ailment and what needs to be done to help with it, Lanitis concludes.

31

Eye–Body Connection

◆

Eyes are a very special part of the body, composed in part of tissue identical to brain tissue and very closely linked to the brain in many functions. Nevertheless, the eyes are connected with the rest of the body by way of blood vessels, nerves and muscles, write Meir Schneider and her researcher colleagues. They simultaneously affect the rest of the body and are affected by it.

Vision problems are very frequently accompanied by specific patterns of muscle tension and weakness. As with other types of physical problems, it is very difficult to say, with accuracy, this tension created that problem or that problem may have caused this tension. This tends to get one involved in an unsolvable, chicken-or-egg type of discussion. Does a person have a tight neck because of myopia, or vice versa? It is not always possible to say. We have seen, however, that the two things always go together.

Massage of the whole face influences the circulation around the eyes. Without even looking at the body of a nearsighted person, one can predict confidently that they will have pronounced tension in the forehead, jaw, neck, shoulders, upper arms, lower back, and often the calves as well. Relaxing these areas will often produce an immediate improvement in vision, and doing vision exercises will often help these areas to relax.

It has been found that a combination of vision exercises, bodywork and body-relaxation exercises is far more effective than simply doing vision exercises alone.

Reducing body tension

Eyestrain and upper-body tension are closely related. Strenuous use of the eyes can set up patterns of tension in the neck, shoulders, arms and other areas. Conversely, muscular tension in these areas can adversely affect the eyes by decreasing circulation to the head, causing a sense of exhaustion in both the eyes and the mind. Anyone whose job involves sitting at a desk, bent over work, may experience this type of tension and exhaustion as a regular part of the job. This position, in which most of us spend from six to eight hours of every workday, creates strain in the back and neck, and tension in the shoulders and arms.

Shoulder rotations are wonderful for releasing shoulder and upper-back tension since they work directly on the shoulder muscles.

One of the reasons people become so fatigued at work is the tendency to work without stopping for anything but food, coffee or a cigarette. We become so engrossed in our work that we can completely ignore our physical discomfort – until we get home.

People often feel pressured to work straight through because of a deadline or a backlog of work. The irony of this is that when we do take a few minutes for a break to rest, stretch, relax – a genuine breathing space – we find ourselves able to accomplish more than we can when we are perpetually driven to exhaustion.

Some employers are recognising this and are providing their workers with a place to rest, even to lie down for a few minutes every so often. Even when a friend worked at a cannery, the workers were given five minutes every hour to go outside on the dock, and she would use the time for sunning or for shoulder rotations or spine stretches. No one thought this was strange; everyone knew that the work made them stiff and uncomfortable.

There is more awareness nowadays that the same can be true of sedentary jobs, particularly if they involve computers. There is a whole science called ergonomics, which is devoted to designing workspaces which won't cripple the workers. Those of us who work at home, however, as well as those of us who do not have enlightened employers, have to look out for our own physical welfare during work.

It is all connected

To understand the eye–body relationship, we need to experience it kinaesthetically. What does seeing feel like? Most of the time we are not aware of it; we feel the effects of seeing only after the fact, in the form of eyestrain, eye fatigue, neck tension and other related problems. It is possible, however, to learn to feel immediately when we strain our eyes or the muscles surrounding them, and to stop ourselves from doing so.

A good place to begin is with the muscles closest to the eyes and most directly affected by seeing – the facial muscles. For many years we have been teaching our vision improvement students to massage their faces, with particular attention to several specific places which seem to have an especially good effect on vision. We have just recently discovered that these are the same points used by the Chinese in acupressure massage – for the same purpose. We are not sure whether this validates their method or ours – probably both. In any case, Meir Schneider highly recommends facial massage, particularly as a preparation for palming. One of the most important functions of palming is, in fact, relaxation of the muscles around the eyes.

Try this exercise: Massage of the whole face influences the circulation around the eyes. So rub your hands together until they are warm, then massage your face with your fingertips, gently at first, and then more firmly, as your muscles also begin to warm up. The pressure at first should be just firm enough to let you feel whether a spot is tense or painful, but not hard enough to make pain worse. Spend at least a couple of minutes on each separate area, noticing how your touch feels and what effect it has. You may feel a deep tension or pain, a superficial tightness, a pleasant sense of release, or numbness, which is also a sensation.

Begin with the jaw. Massage the whole area from the point of the chin outward along the jawbone, in front of and behind the ears. You can open and close your jaws while doing this, to help stretch and relax the strong jaw muscles. This may make you feel like yawning, so yawn as much as you want – it is very relaxing for your face.

Now work up from the bridge of the nose outward along the cheekbones towards the temples. From the bridge of the nose, work out along the eyebrows, massaging above, below and directly on the brow. Spend a little extra time on the point between the eyebrows; this area gathers a lot of tension from the act of seeing. Then massage in long firm strokes across the forehead and, very gently, with small circular motions, in the temple area. Stroke lightly from the temples up into your scalp, imagining that you are drawing tension away from your eyes.

After ten minutes or so of massage, your face will be glowing and tingling from the increased blood flow. Besides increasing the kinaesthetic sense of your eyes, these exercises strengthen the tissues around the eyes. Move both eyes simultaneously in small circles. If you need to, you can hold up a finger before your eyes and move it in a circle, allowing the eye to follow it, but first see if you can move the eyes in rotation without this aid. Touch your forehead above the eyes with your fingertips.

Can you feel the muscles moving? They do not need to. Try to relax them and practise this exercise until you can do it without working the forehead muscles. You may simply need to make your circles smaller; in fact, see how small you can make them. Close your eyes and visualise them moving in circles, freely, with no effort. It may help to picture a wheel rolling, or a record on a turntable, or something else that turns smoothly and easily. With your eyes open, rotate them again, and this time imagine that only the pupils are rotating.

Now close your eyes and move them in rotation under the closed lids. This may be more difficult, since the movement is so much more limited. Touch your eyeballs lightly as you do this, to feel the movement. Notice whether you tense the rest of your face during this motion; if you do, try not to.

You will find it much easier to do this exercise with your eyes open after this. Working on your vision demands a high level of awareness, and it will be enormously helpful to you if you begin your vision work in a state of attunement with your body.

32
Tension Headaches

◆

The remedies presented here have been extracted from the book: *The One Minute (or so) Healer*, by Dan Ullman, M.Ph. While we present just ten suggestions here, the book contains nineteen one-minute strategies for headaches. Approximately 90 per cent of headaches are tension headaches, but perhaps they should be called "tension neck and backaches" because it is the tightening of the neck and back muscles that usually creates the pain in the head.

Tension headaches seem to be an equal-opportunity affliction. They can be caused by almost any type of stress: too much or too little exertion, too much or too little excitement, too hot or too cold temperatures, too much or too little sleep, too erect or too limp a posture, too much or too little food, and so on.

Tension headaches can lead to irresponsible behaviour, which can actually have a real practical value. You may tell your spouse, "I can't do the dishes, honey." You may tell your employer, "I can't finish that project." You may tell your children, "Shut up and stop having fun." This selfish behaviour might lead you to rest and take care of your headache. Sometimes it seems that a headache is nature's way of getting you to relax.

If, however, your teeth are clenched so tightly that people think you are doing a Clint Eastwood impersonation, if your neck is so tight that industry wants to patent this musculature, or if your eyeballs hurt when you move them, then you are paying the price of not resting and enjoying yourself enough. You now have some catch-up to do.

If your eyes are not cooperating with you because of a headache, get someone to read the following strategies to you.

Don't relax... at least not yet

An effective technique for reducing tension headaches is to tighten muscles in the head, neck and jaw for five to ten seconds... and then release them. You may find that you will be able to achieve a deeper level of relaxation from this simple exercise.

Get in touch with the temples

Remember the old aspirin commercials showing a furrow-browed man with an awful headache? As you may recall, he is seen massaging his temples. There are important acupressure points at the temples that are often effective for relieving tension. Place four fingers (not the thumb) along both temples and do a circular massaging motion. Massage for a minute...

Head to acupressure

The head and neck are full of invaluable acupressure points that can release tension when they are pressed firmly. Search your head and neck for "hot" points – that is, points that seem to be sensitive to pressure. Press them for at least five seconds, relax for five seconds, and repeat several times.

Your head is in your hands

There is an acupressure point just barely below the nail of your middle finger. If your pain is primarily on one side, then press the point on that side's hand, and if on both sides, then alternate pressing each hand.

Head for the herbs

Various herbal teas can help you relax. Place a tablespoon each of chamomile and skullcap into a cup of boiling water and let it steep for five minutes. Another good combination of herbs is one teaspoon each of hops and peppermint, and two teaspoons each of chamomile, rosemary and wood betony.

Support your head

Evening primrose oil and gingko help improve circulation to the head and can help reduce headache pain. Take 500 mg of primrose oil and gingko tablets three times a day.

A bright idea

Cool-white fluorescent lights, which are commonly used in many businesses, give some people headaches. Ask your employer to help enhance worker health and productivity by replacing these bulbs with full-spectrum lighting.

Watch funny movies

Laughter releases tension. You may laugh your headache off.

Play a different game

Tension headaches can result from an over-competitive personality.

Create win–win situations. Appreciate the art of losing. Honour the quality of the performance, not simply the first prize.

33
Ageing Gracefully

◆

"The ways in which we currently age have been programmed into us, and we have accepted this idea as a reality," writes Louise L. Hay. As a society, with some exceptions we have come to believe that we all will get old, sick, senile, frail and die – in that order. This does not have to be the truth for us any longer.

As we refuse to accept these old fears and beliefs, this can become a time for us to begin to reverse the negative parts of the ageing process. The current crop of baby boomers is not going to sit back and age like their parents did. We will live longer, and if we take charge of our health we will live exciting, productive lives, Hay writes. "I believe that the second half of our lives can be even more wonderful than the first half – we can definitely make these years exciting ones." If we want to age successfully, then we must make a conscious choice to do so. Healthy ageing is learning how to keep the life force strong within us. We can do this with self-love and with good food and exercise. Staying healthy into our later years is an act of loving ourselves. We can make deliberate choices to care for who we are. We can study books on nutrition in order to learn to fuel our bodies with the most nutritious foods possible. I don't like to talk about diet; rather, I choose to talk about food choices. We can explore some form of exercise to keep our bones strong and our bodies flexible. We can read books, or listen to tapes, or take classes that teach us how to use our minds.

We can learn how to think in ways that support a peaceful, loving, healthy life.

"Whenever I see older people who are frail, ill and incapacitated, I know I am often looking at a lifetime of inadequate nutrition, lack of exercise and an accumulation of years of negative thoughts and beliefs," Hay writes. "So many of the problems we face in our later years come from the lifestyle choices we made when we were younger. We need to learn how to take care of our magnificent bodies so that we can sail into our older years in perfect physical shape. I had a physical recently and the doctor told me I was in amazingly good physical condition for someone my age. It disturbed me that he expected a woman of seventy-two to be in poor health."

Living a healthful life

Fast food and processed packaged foods do not support life. No matter how pretty and mouth-watering the picture on the package, there is no life in these foods. Our bodies need fresh, living foods, such as fresh fruits, salads, vegetables, grains; and small amounts of meats, poultry and fish. These are the foods that will sustain our bodies well into old age. You may not want to hear this, but deep fried food is also "heart attack food". It may please the taste buds, but eaten consistently over a lifetime it contributes to all sorts of health problems.

As teenagers, we can get away with a lot of poor food choices. We may not feel our best, but at least we're not sick. However, when we reach our mid-forties, our past food history begins to catch up with us. This is when so many women find that their bodies are not working well, and the diseases start to manifest.

Do not listen to the dairy or meat industries. They do not care about your health; they are only interested in profits. Eating lots of red meat and dairy products is not good for anyone's bodies. Caffeine and sugar are two other culprits that contribute to many of the problems that we face with our health.

Ask yourself, "How do I want to age?" Hay suggests that we closely observe people who are ageing miserably and notice those who are ageing magnificently. What do these two groups do differently? Are you willing to do what it takes to be healthy, happy and fulfilled in your later years?

Almost all the research done on older people has been by the pharmaceutical industry on disease and what is "wrong" with us and what drugs we require. There is a need to do in-depth studies on older people who are healthy, happy, fulfilled and enjoying their lives. The more we study what is "right" with older people, the more we will know how we can all accomplish healthy living.

How to accept and love our bodies

It is crucial to our wellbeing to constantly love and appreciate ourselves. Loving our bodies is important at any stage of our lives, but it is absolutely vital as we grow older. Anger is not healing. If we put anger into any part of our bodies, especially a part that is sick, it only delays the healing process. If there is some part of your body that you are not happy with, then take a month or so and put love into that area on a daily basis. Tell your body that you love it: "I love you, body! I really, really love you!"

What if part of your body is sagging or wrinkled? This part has been with you for a lifetime, and it is doing the best it can with the health choices you have made. Hating your body will not make it young and beautiful. Love your body and it will love you back. Your hips and breasts and your face and your skin will be with you for the rest of your life. Take care of your body, and love every bit of it – from the top of your head down to the tips of your toes – and all the organs in between. When you love yourself, others love you, too, and you will be irresistibly attractive all your life.

"I am a great believer in the philosophy that our thoughts and our words shape our experiences. So we can quite unknowingly, just by thinking, contribute to our health or to our diseases." Dr Candace Pert discovered neuropeptides. These are the chemical messengers in our brain that travel to every part of our body, touching every cell and depositing a bit of that chemical in it. They do this each time we think a thought or speak a word, says Hay. "If our thoughts are fearful, angry or in any way negative, then the chemicals these messengers deposit 'depress' our immune systems. If our thoughts are loving, optimistic and positive, then the different chemicals these messengers, or neuropeptides, deposit will 'enhance' our immune systems."

So, moment by moment, we are consciously or unconsciously choosing healthy thoughts or unhealthy thoughts. Poisonous thoughts poison our bodies. We cannot allow ourselves to indulge in negative thinking. It is making us sick and killing us.

In addition to making sound choices for ourselves nutritionally and medically, we need to take charge of our thinking. Negative thinking produces negative experiences. If we want to change our lives for the better, we must learn to think thoughts that support us and help improve the quality of our lives. When we love and appreciate who we are, we naturally take better care of ourselves.

34
10 Ways to Better Health Now!

Dr Elson Haas recommends the following ways to better health:
1. Chew your food well and take time to nourish yourself. Eat a balanced diet of wholesome, natural foods.
2. Drink one to two glasses of good water several times a day; first thing in the morning and about half an hour before meals are the best times.
3. Eat only as much as you need and very little after nightfall, and definitely not much at all within two or three hours before sleep.
4. Exercise regularly, finding a balance of strengthening, stretching and aerobic activities.
5. Sleep well, and at least 6–8 hours nightly as your body seems to require.
6. Relax and let go of stressful thoughts and frustrating emotions.
7. Communicate both your thoughts and your feelings clearly with your friends, co-workers and loved ones.
8. Say things out of love, not anger, when you have differences with another; remember your words can hurt.
9. Keep your attitude UP and try to see the best in your work and your life; if things are not going well, apply yourself to improving them.
10. LOVE YOURSELF and let love in your life; learn to express the wonderful ways you feel about everyone around you!